William Denton, Elodie Lawton Mijatovic

Serbian Folklore

Second Edition

William Denton, Elodie Lawton Mijatovic

Serbian Folklore

Second Edition

ISBN/EAN: 9783744767996

Printed in Europe, USA, Canada, Australia, Japan

Cover: Foto ©ninafisch / pixelio.de

More available books at **www.hansebooks.com**

SERBIAN FOLK-LORE

LONDON:
THE COLUMBUS PRINTING, PUBLISHING AND ADVERTISING COMPANY, LIMITED,
AMBERLEY HOUSE, NORFOLK STREET, W.C.

SERBIAN FOLK-LORE

TRANSLATED FROM THE SERBIAN

By MADAME ELODIE L. MIJATOVICH

AUTHOR OF THE "HISTORY OF MODERN SERBIA," "KOSSOVO BALLADS"
ETC. ETC. ETC.

WITH AN INTRODUCTION

By THE LATE REV. W. DENTON, M.A.

SECOND EDITION

1899

THE COLUMBUS PRINTING, PUBLISHING AND ADVERTISING COMPANY,
LIMITED,
AMBERLEY HOUSE, NORFOLK STREET, W.C.

Preparing for Publication,

SERBIAN POPULAR CUSTOMS,

A Further Contribution to Serbian Folk-Lore,

BY MADAME ELODIE L. MIJATOVICH.

CONTENTS.

	PAGE.
INTRODUCTION	1
THE BEAR'S SON	23
THE WONDERFUL KIOSK	31
THE SNAKE'S GIFT. LANGUAGE OF ANIMALS	36
THE GOLDEN APPLE-TREE, AND THE NINE PEAHENS	42
PAPALLUGA ; OR, THE GOLDEN SLIPPER	58
THE GOLDEN-FLEECED RAM	65
WHO ASKS LITTLE, GETS MUCH	74
JUSTICE OR INJUSTICE ? WHICH IS BEST	80
SATAN'S JUGGLINGS AND GOD'S MIGHT	84
THE WISE GIRL	88
GOOD DEEDS ARE NEVER LOST	93
LYING FOR A WAGER	103
THE WICKED STEPMOTHER	108
BIRD GIRL	114
SIR PEPPERCORN	117
BASH-CHALEK ; OR, TRUE STEEL	139
THE SHEPHERD AND THE KING'S DAUGHTER	165
ONE GOOD TURN DESERVES ANOTHER	180
THE BITER BIT	191

	PAGE
THE TRADE THAT NO ONE KNOWS	206
THE THREE SUITORS	221
THE GOLDEN-HAIRED TWINS	228
THE DREAM OF THE KING'S SON	237
THE THREE BROTHERS	245
ANIMALS AS FRIENDS AND AS ENEMIES	282
THE LEGEND OF ST. GEORGE	295

INTRODUCTION.

IT is only within the last few years that the importance of folk-lore, the popular legends, tales, drolls, and extravagances which have been handed down from generation to generation among the labourers, peasants and youth of a nation, has been frankly recognised. It is now, however, generally acknowledged that this kind of literature, which more than all other deserves the name of popular, possesses a value beyond any momentary amusement which the tales themselves may afford, and it has assumed an honourable post side by side with other and graver materials, and has obtained a recognised use in deciding the conclusions of the historian and ethnologist. It is fortunate that the utility of these 'tales and old wives' fables' should have been thus recognised, otherwise the dull utilitarianism of modern educators would soon have trampled out these fragments of the 'elder time,' and have left to our children no alternative than that of 'being crammed with geography and natural history.'* The collection of Serbian popular tales, now translated into English and here published, is an additional contribution to our knowledge of such literature—the most venerable secular literature, it may be, which has come down to our times.

At the wish of the lady who has selected and translated these tales, I have undertaken to edit them. In doing so I have, however, preserved, as far as possible, the literality of her version, and have limited myself to the addition of a few notes to the text. The tales included in this volume have been selected from two collections of Serbian folk-lore; the greater part from the well-known 'Srpske narodne pripovijetke,' of Vuk Stefanovich Karadjich, published at Vienna, in 1853, and others from the 'Bosniacke narodne pripovijetke,' collected by the 'Society of Young Bosnia,' the first part of which collection was printed at Sissek, in Croatia, in 1870. The collection of Vuk Stefanovich Karadjich was translated into German by his daughter Wilhelmina, and printed at Berlin, in 1854.† To this volume, which is dedicated to the Princess Julia, widow of the late Prince Michel Obrenovich III., Jacob Grimm, who suggested to Karadjich the utility of making the original collection, has contributed a short but interesting preface.

The collection of Vuk Karadjich was gathered by him from the lips of professional story-tellers, and of

* Charles Lamb, in a letter to Coleridge October, 1802.
† 'Volksmärchen der Serben, gesammelt und herausgegeben von Vuk Stephanowitsch Karadschitsch.' Berlin, 1854.

INTRODUCTION. 3

old peasant women in Serbia and the Herzegovina. One of these stories, translated in the present volume, and here called 'The Wonderful Kiosk,' or 'The Kiosk in the Sky,' was however written out and contributed to this collection by Prince Michael, the late and lamented ruler of Serbia, who had heard it, in childhood, from the lips of his nurse. The Bosniac collection was made by young theological students from that country—members of the college at Dyakovo, in Croatia.

The taste for this species of literature has, during the last few years, led to the publication of various collections of traditional folk-tales, legends, and sagas, from all countries including and lying between Iceland and the southern extremity of Africa and of Polynesia, until a very ample body of such stories have been made accessible even to the mere English reader. Whilst Mr. Thorpe* and Mr. Dasent† have directed their attention to Iceland and the Scandinavian kingdoms, Mr. Campbell has rendered important service by his large collection of West Highland stories.‡ Indian legends, and folk-lore in general, has been illustrated by the volumes of Mr. W. H. Wilson, Dr. Muir,§, Colonel Jacob, Mr. Kelly‖, and Miss Frere¶; and the Cingalese traditions by the writings of Mr. Turnour, and especially

* 'Northern Mythology,' 3 vols.
† 'Popular Tales from the Norse.'
‡ 'Popular Tales of the West Highlands,' 4 vols. Edinb. 1860—62.
§ 'Original Sanskrit Texts on the Origin and History of the People of India, &c.'
‖ 'Indo-European Traditions.'
¶ 'Old Deccan Days.'

by the volumes of Mr. Spence Hardy.* Russian and North Slavonic folk-lore has been made accessible and arranged in the valuable volumes of Mr. Ralston, on 'The Songs of the Russian People,' and on 'Russian Folk-Lore.' Dr. Bleek has collected some of the myths and popular tales of the tribes in the neighbourhood of the Cape of Good Hope†; and Sir George Grey has done the same good service in preserving specimens of the folk-tales of the people of New Zealand.‡ Whilst foreign countries have given up their stores of popular literature to these investigations, similar industry has been shown in collecting the traditions and folk-lore of our own country. The songs collected in Sir Walter Scott's 'Border Minstrelsy', illustrated as they are by the notes which he added, are a store-house alike for the northern counties of England and the southern counties of Scotland. Mr. Wright and Mr. Cockayne, in their volumes, that on the 'Literature of the Middle Ages,' by the former gentleman, and that of the 'Leechdoms of Early England,' by the latter, have brought together the folk-lore of our forefathers; and in the pages of Baker§, Chambers‖, Hone¶, Henderson**, Hunt††, and others, are stored up much of the local folk-lore and

   * 'Manual of Buddhism, and 'Legends and Theories of the Buddhists.' London. 1866.
   † 'Reynard, the Fox, in South Africa,'
   ‡ 'Polynesian Mythology and Traditions of New Zealand,'
   § 'Folk-Lore of Northamptonshire.'
   ‖ 'The Book of Days.'
   ¶ 'Table Book' and 'Year Book.'
   ** 'Notes on the Folk-Lore of the Northern Counties of England and the Borders.'
   †† 'Drolls of Old Cornwall.' 2 vols.

tales which still exist amongst us, and which we have inherited from our Aryan ancestors,—echoes of stories first heard by them in their home in Central Asia.

By means of these and similar collections, we are enabled to trace and compare the folk-tale in the various stages of its growth, and note its modifications, according to the religion of the people who have received it, and the climate of the countries in which it has been naturalised. In the pages of Professor Max Müller, of Mr. Baring Gould, and of Mr. Cox, we have attempts, more or less successful, to treat these stories scientifically, and to trace and explain the origin and motive of the various popular tales and legends which are conprehended under the name of folk-lore.

An examination of these collections leads to the conclusion that—apart at least from the legends of history —the number of strictly original folk-tales is but small; and that people, settled for ages in countries separated geographically, have yet possessed from remote antiquity a popular literature, which must have been the common property of the race before it branched into nations; but that the natural accretions, the growth of time, together with local colouring, fragments of historical facts, the influence of popular religious belief, and, above all, the exigencies and ingenuity of professional story-tellers, have so modified these primitive tales and legends, that an appearance of originality has been imparted to current popular tales, which, however, a larger acquaintance with folk-lore, and a more extended investigation, are now gradually dispelling. It is at length evident that various primitive legendary and traditionary elements have been combined in most of these tales; and that the only originality consists in such combination. They resemble a piece of tesselated work made up of cubes of coloured stone, the tints of which are really few in number, though they admit of being arranged into a variety of figures after the fancy of the artist.

In the appendix to Mr. Henderson's 'Notes on the Folk-Lore of the Northern Counties of England,' under the appropriate name of 'Story-radicals,' the reader will find a useful and suggestive classification of the elements which enter into the composition of various popular tales borrowed from Von Hahn's introduction to his collection of Greek and Albanian folk-tales; and although this classification is rendered imperfect by the recent large increase of such stories, yet it suffices to explain the manner in which fragments selected from other popular fictions have been built up and agglutinated together. Philological research is day by day illustrating more clearly the original oneness of the language of mankind; and collections of household stories and popular legends are showing that much of the really popular literature, especially such as lingers in lands uninvaded by modern civilisation, and in sequestered spots in the midst of such civilisation, was possessed in common, before mankind was parted off into races, and subdivided into tribes and nations; so that they also furnish another proof of the unity of the human race. We are still able, at least to some extent, to trace the genealogy of many popular stories, and to ascend to their fountain-head, or at least to such a distance as to indicate the time when they originated, and the land where they were first told. Thus we may feel sure that had some of the tales in this volume been the original fancies of Slavonic minstrels and storytellers they would not have been garnished with crocodiles, alligators, elephants, and the fauna and flora of Hindoostan, and that the germ of such stories must therefore have existed before the Slav made his home in Europe. Such accessories are sufficient proof that the tales themselves could not have been indigenous to the banks of the Danube, but must have been brought thither by a race which had migrated from a more southern and eastern home.

Whilst the original home of these stories may thus be satisfactorily proved to have been in other lands than that in which they are now found, the growth of the tale, story, legend, or droll may be traced by an examination of the stories themselves. They are, in most instances, composite—an agglutination of fragments such as is seen in the breccias and similar stones of igneous origin. The desire of being credited with originality—a common weakness of humanity—the necessity of lengthening out a tale so as to fill up a definite amount of time in its recitation, and the wish to amuse by novel combinations—all tended to the structural growth of these tales. This was effected in part by the unexpected arrangements of old and wellknown incidents, in part by the easier and coarser expedient of mere repetition. Thus, a common trick of the story-teller was to repeat all the details of the events which happened to one of the personages in his story, and to attribute them to each of the three, or even the seven heroes who had started in search of adventures, and whom he makes meet with precisely similar fortunes. These repetitions sometimes appear and are sometimes dispensed with, according to the exigencies of time, or the skill of the narrator. The other expedient of adding to the original tale incidents taken from other stories, admits of the exercise of much ingenuity on the part of the story-teller, and entitled him, in some degree, to the credit of originality. The fact remains, however, that the materials out of which such stories are constructed are less numerous than the stories themselves; which have for thousands of years delighted and amused, and sometimes instructed, both old and young alike, the peasant and the prince, the rude Hottentot of Southern Africa, the stolid boor of Russia, and the quick-witted and intelligent Greek.

It is comparatively an easy task to trace the popular stories which are familiar to us, to the countries where they were originally told; or, at least, to decide approximately as to the land of their birth. Still more easy to decompose them, and separate the original germ from the accretions which have gathered around it in its course. It is not so easy, however, to determine the motive of the original story. According to one school of writers, these popular folk-tales embody profound mythological dogmas, and were even purposely constructed to convey, by means of symbolical or histrionic teaching, the maxims of ancient religions and philosophies. To some extent this is possibly true; apart, however, from the fact, and the speculations which the facts may give rise to, the truth or falsity of this is of but little practical value. No skill which we possess can decide with any certainty as to the mythological or non-mythological origin of a folk-tale, or families of such tales, and the attempts which have been made to interpret such tales in accordance with mythology, have ended in absurd failures.

Much confusion of thought, as it appears to me, exists as to the mythological motive which is claimed for many of these folk-tales; and men have confounded the mythological explanation of a tale with its mythological origin and motive. We shall, however, have done but little in the way of clearing up this question when we have adjusted the various incidents of a folk-tale to the teaching of ancient mythology. The attempt to do so resembles the labours of the neo-Platonic expounders of declining Paganism, in their endeavours to make it appear more reasonable by giving to the gross and material incidents of ancient polytheism a subtle and recondite spiritual interpretation. The question— too frequently lost sight of—being not whether the incidents of Pagan mythology might by any such process be reconciled with the intellect of a philosopher, but whether the incidents themselves originated in the intent to present spiritual truth to the mind, and were bodied forth in order to convey such spiritual lessons to the apprehension of the worshipper. There is a similar order to be observed in the examination and interpretation of these tales; and the most ingenious interpretation of a folk-tale, and its adjustment to the incidents of mythology, do not advance us one step towards determining its motive, and clearing up the obscurities which surround its origin. Again, the presence of mythological incidents in a tale in no degree accounts for its origin; nor does it assist us in proving these tales to possess a mythological character. In popular literature—especially in such a literature as that of which I am speaking—the tone of the popular mind must needs be reflected; and if mythology had, at the date of the creation of the tale, or during its growth, any considerable hold over the popular mind, this fact would be indicated by the characters introduced, as well as by the general colouring given to the tale itself; just as a profoundly religious mind tinges the creations of the imagination or the productions of the intellect with the religious convictions which possess it. But tales and scientific treatises may be profoundly Christian in their *ethos*, without it being necessary for us to attribute to their authors the intention of presenting, by this means, an esoteric explanation of the articles of the Creed.

Now it is to be borne in mind, that at the time when most of the primary materials, out of which these folk-tales are constructed, originated, polytheism had peopled the groves and streams, the mountains and the valleys, the hills and plains, the sky above and the deep sea below, and even the centre of the earth, with supernatural beings. Every day and every fraction of life had its tutelary; every family its special *lar*; and every individual its *genius*, or guardian spirit. Omnipresence was subdivided into atoms, and an atom was everywhere present. Under such circumstances it would hardly have been possible to construct a tale or to rearrange the fragments of older tales without introducing these elements of the popular belief. Without doing so, indeed, a tale would not—could not have become a folk-tale. This, however, in no way makes probable the mythological signification and origin of such tales, any more than the introduction of guns and pistols, of gas or the telegraph, into a modern tale, would prove it to have a military or a scientific motive.

A specimen of the way in which folk-tales are interpreted mythologically will, I think, show at once the ingenuity of the interpreter and the baselessness of the interpretation. The tale which I cite as a specimen of this kind of treatment is one which, like folk-tales in general, occurs in several forms in England, in Southern Italy, in Germany, in the Tyrol, in Hungary, in Iceland, Swabia, Wallachia, and Greece, and probably in other countries. I give it in the form in which it appears in the 'Modern Greek Household Tales,' edited by Von Hahn, because the Greek version of this tale has the merit of being 'shorter than most of its variants.' The ingenious though fanciful explanation will be found in the appendix to Mr. Henderson's

'Notes on the Folk-Lore of the Northern Counties of England':—

'A man and a woman had no children; the woman prayed that she might be granted one, even though it were a serpent; and in due course of time she brought forth a serpent, which left the house and took up its abode in a hole.

'The woman is a terrible shrew, and a bad woman to boot; she brings the house to poverty, and then goes to the serpent to ask for relief. The serpent gives his mother a gold-dropping ass, warning her never to let it touch water. The couple live on the gold for some while, but at last the woman leads the ass to the water, and it runs away and is lost. She goes once more to her child, who gives her a pitcher, which does all she wants; she sells this to the king, and is reduced to poverty. The old man now goes to the serpent's lair and obtains a stick, to which he says, "Up stick, and do your duty!" whereupon it knocks the woman on the head and kills her; so the man lives in happiness ever after.'

On this, the writer who undertakes to interpret this tale observes—

'That these stories rest upon a common mythological foundation, there is strong evidence to prove. The gold-dropping animal, the magic table or napkin, the self-acting cudgel, appear in some of the tales of ancient India, and their original signification is made apparent.

'The master, who gives the three precious gifts, is the All Father—the Supreme Spirit. The gold and jewel dropping ass is the spring cloud hanging in the sky, and shedding the bright productive Vernal showers. The table which covers itself is the earth becoming covered with flowers and fruit at the bidding of the New Year. But there is a check; rain is withheld, the process of vegetation is stayed, by some evil influence. Then comes the Thunder cloud, out of which leaps the bolt and rains pour down, the earth receives them, and is covered with abundance—all that was lost is restored.'

The incident of the dropping of jewels only appears in the Neapolitan version, given in the 'Pentamerone' of Giambattista Basile,* and is apparently an addition made by him to the original story. The explanation of the meaning of the tale, it appears to me, might as fittingly have been taken from the region of science, or of history, and might have been as easily interpreted in a thousand and one other ways as in this. So that if, originally, the folk-tale embodied a mythological truth, which, however, may be affirmed or denied with equal right, the fact is of no value in aiding us to determine what the intentions of the inventor of the tale must have been.

Mythological symbolism, like very much of what passes current as ecclesiastical symbolism, is a testimony to the ingenuity of the interpreter; it has, oftentimes, no existence in the object interpreted. We may, to our own satisfaction, perhaps, resolve the sternest facts into impalpable fancies; the fact remains, and will

* Naples, 1837.

remain when the fancy has faded into its original nothingness or lingers only as a beautiful freak of fancy. The twelve Cæsars were living and historical personages, though an ingenious apologist has reduced them into mythological non-existences, and has traced in them a likeness to the twelve signs of the Zodiac. Mythological and legendary incidents, it is true, have a tendency to fasten themselves upon real men and women until, like parasitical plants round the trunk of a tree, they conceal the true character of those who are thus clothed. Sir Richard Whittington, however, was Lord Mayor of London, though the sounds heard from the brow of Highgate Hill—

> 'When he, a friendless and a drooping boy,
> Sat on a stone, and heard the bells speak out—
> Articulate music '—*

had no more real existence than his famous cat, and though we are indebted for the means by which his great wealth was acquired only to the pleasant invention of the popular-romance writer.

Probably many of these stories possess an historical origin, and could we recover their original form, they might be found to record real incidents in the life of an historical personage or of a nation. The original form, however, can now hardly be even guessed at. Successive generations of story-tellers have added to the original tale, and have changed archaic incidents for those better understood by the audience, and therefore

* Wordsworth, ' The Prelude.'

appealing the readier to their sympathies. When transplanted from its home to a distant land the local colouring has been changed, unintelligible customs have been made to give place to vernacular ones, until so little remains of the old tale that even with the help of comparative analysis it is now impossible to recover the form in which it was given out at the first. Even with a written literature and with diffused information, Shakespeare found it necessary to the stories which he dramatized to interweave appliances made known by modern discoveries, and, accordingly, anachronisms abound in his plays. If this has been the case even where the national literature was a written one, we might be confident beforehand that we should find the story-teller of the Southern Slavs lengthening out and giving variety to his tale, not from the stores of archæology, but from such common, every-day customs as would appeal forcibly to his simple audience.

The reader who is familiar with the stories accumulated by recent collectors, will trace, without difficulty, in the present volume, those fragments of the primary tales out of which story-tellers in all parts of the world have for many generations constructed or expanded their own tales. It is, therefore, unnecessary for me to do this. I add, however, a few notices of some of the tales included in this volume, merely as illustrations of the way in which they have been built up out of older materials: like the palaces of the modern Roman nobility, out of the marbles which were originally intended to perpetuate the memory of the victories of the Republic and the magnificence of the ministers of the Empire.

In the tale which is entitled 'Justice or Injustice,'* the manner in which the king's daughter is enticed on ship-board, and carried off with her attendant maidens, will at once recall the incident related in the opening paragraph of the history of Herodotus. The resemblance between the narrative of the abduction of the daughter of Inachus by the Phœnician merchants, and that in the tale, is so close that it can hardly be accidental. Some will think that this lends some support to the notion that the account in Herodotus is mythological; others that the Serb tale is probably based on an historical fact. That the tale in this volume is not of Serbian origin, is evident from the introduction of the elephants, and the description of their capture after being intoxicated. The restoration of the hero by means of 'the water of life,' is an incident common to very many of these folk-tales, and may fairly be regarded as a 'story-radical.' In the tale of 'Bash Chalek,' this water of life is changed and christianized into 'the water of Jordan,' whereas in its North Slavonic variant it is still the 'water of life' which is retained as the means by which the hero is recalled from death. In most particulars the Serbian tale closely follows the Russian type, and may be compared with the tale which Mr. Ralston has translated under the title of 'Marya Morevna.'† The 'True Steel' of the

* Ralston's 'Russian Folk-Tales,' p. 85.
† Ralston's 'Russian Folk-Tales,' p. 85.

Serbian tale is the Koshchei the Deathless of the Russian story; and the younger brother of the North Slavonic story is evidently the Prince Ivan of the South Slavonic tale. Again, two of the wooers are the same in both stories, the chief variation being that in the Serbian folk-tale the raven is introduced instead of the dragon of the Russian story.

The Bosniac story of 'The Three Brothers' is a good example of the way in which the expansion of these stories is effected. We have here three separate stories thrown into one; the various incidents of which are to be sought for in a variety of tales and in different countries. In part the tale seems to be an echo of the Egyptian story, which, written on papyrus and believed to be of the date of the Exodus of the Israelites, is preserved in the Bibliothèque Impériale. Of this story, Mr. Goodwin has given an abstract in the Cambridge Essays of 1858. The astonishing leap made by the horse of the younger brother is but an exaggeration of the sufficiently exaggerated exploit of Buddha's horse, Kantako, which was thirty-six feet long, was able to go three hundred miles in one night, and, when impeded by the Déwas, overcame the obstacles interposed in the way of its progress by leaping across the river Anoma, a distance of two hundred and ten feet.* In part, however, the details of this part of the story accords with the account of the leap made by the horse Rama Rajah which took three successive leaps, not only over a wide river, but

* Hardy's 'Legends and Theories of the Buddhists,' p. 134.

also over four thick and tall groves of copal, soparee, guava, and cocoa-nut trees, as told in the story of 'Rama and Luxman.'* Again, the iron teeth of the sister in the Bosniac story make part of the marvels in the Russian story of 'The Witch,'† and has its counterpart in the incident of the Syriote story of 'The Striga.'‡ The way in which the old woman destroys her victims by throwing around them a hair of her head is also common to these folk-tales, and to several which may be found in the collections of similar tales told in widely separated countries.

The incident of the tree growing out of the grave in the Serb story of 'The Golden-haired Twins,' makes also part of the story of 'Punchkin' in the collection of stories from the Deccan, where a pomelo tree which springs from the grave of a murdered person leads to the knowledge of the murder.§ The same incident again occurs in 'Truth's Triumph' in the same collection,¶ where the hundred and one children of the king and Guzra Bai, after having been destroyed by the ranee, their stepmother, and buried by her orders, have their grave marked by a tree springing spontaneously from it; and when the mango tree has been cut down by the orders of the ranee and directed to be burnt, a sudden rising of the water prevents the order from being carried out, and the trunk is floated down to a place of

---

* Frere's 'Old Deccan Days,' p. 76.
† Ralston's 'Russian Folk-Tales,' p. 163.
‡ Hahn's 'Modern Greek Household Tales,' No. lxv.
§ 'Old Deccan Days,' p. 4.
¶ *Ibid*, p. 54.

security, stranded on a bank, and again changed into children.

Another of what I have ventured to call 'primitive fragments,' because commonly made use of in the construction of the folk-tales of various races, makes its appearance in the story of 'The Biter Bit.' In that story the giant demands as his reward that he should receive what the old man had 'forgotten at home;' and obtains one of his sons, who had been left behind when his numerous brothers had set out on their bride-seeking expedition. This reappears in the Russian tale of 'The Water King and Vasilissa the Wise,'* and also in the story of 'The Youth' from the same lands.† The latter part of the story resembles the incidents in the Indian tale of 'Sringabhuja.' In 'Peppercorn' the episode of the maces which the hero requires, and with which he is unsatisfied until the third has been made to stand the test of being thrown into the air and descending on the forehead of 'Peppercorn' without breaking the mace, but merely bruising the forehead of the hero, occurs not only in the Serbian tale of 'The Bear's Son,' but also the Russian story of 'Ivan Popyalof,' of which Mr. Ralston has given us a translation; whilst the fraud practised on 'Peppercorn' by his two companions who leave him in the deep hole down which he has descended, and his subsequent adventures both below and on the earth, are almost identical with incidents in another Russian folk-tale, 'The Norka.'‡

* Ralston's 'Russian Folk-Tales,' p. 120.
† Ibid, p. 139.
‡ Ibid, p. 73.

I have noted these various resemblances and borrowings, or rather variations from one and the same original, because they illustrate the way in which the tales found in all parts of the world have been built up of fragments which are the common property of mankind. I have not thought it necessary to trace out all the resemblances to other tales—all the borrowings from the common stock. Most of my readers will be able to do that for themselves. I have but adduced them by way of example of story-building. They, however, show us that the stock of original materials out of which these folk-tales have been constructed is, comparatively speaking, of but limited extent, and also that the large number of tales which compose the popular literature of the world are but evidences of the skill with which these scanty materials have been combined by the folk-teachers. The literature of a nation is after all but the result of the combination of some five-and-twenty sounds and letters.

In Serbia there is a curious distinction in the use of prose and rhythm in these folk-stories. Prose is the vehicle for tales related by women; rhythm the prerogative of men. Prose stories are usually told in the domestic circle, and in gatherings of women at Selo or Prelo. During the summer evenings when field labour and household occupations have come to a close, it was, and indeed still is, customary in Serbian villages for young girls, accompanied by some older female friends, to gather in groups under the branches of some widespreading tree, and then, whilst the younger people occupy themselves in spinning, some of the older women interest the rest of the company by relating these traditionary stories. Men are excluded from these gatherings, and the story-telling which fills up the chief part of these evenings is looked on as exclusively a feminine occupation. These stories are always in prose.

There are, indeed, men story-tellers. Their tales or stories, however, invariably assume the character of poems, and they are generally—indeed almost always—accompanied by the monotonous sounds of the "gusle." Generally speaking, these poems relate to historical or mythical incidents in the life of the nation; though sometimes they are of the same kind as the folk-tales which are given in this volume, and which are related in the feminine circle. When this is the case the distinction already noted is, however, strictly observed. The folk-tale related by a woman is in prose; the same tale told by a man is cast into the form of a poem. Even the purely Christian legends, of which the reader is presented in this volume with a specimen popular in Bosnia and the Herzégovina, 'The Legend of St. George,' is related with the aid of rhythm. Legends of the latter kind may have been, as some suppose, originally related by priests in their churches, and possibly in prose. Now, however, that they have passed into the possession of the professional story-tellers they have put on the masculine garb of verse. This Homeric feature of Serb customs is indeed now dying out with other national peculiarities. It is, however, far from being dead, nor are such verses employed only in celebrating the glories of the reign of Stephen Dushan, the heroism of George Brankovich, or the mournful defeat of Kossovo. Long tedious debates in the National Parliament, or Skoupshtina, of 1870, on the liberty of opening and keeping shops in villages as distinguished from towns, were summed up and reported throughout the country in a way which would astonish the readers of the debates in our English Parliament. The whole discussion, with the arguments of the various speakers, took the form of a long song or poem, which was recited in the open air before the villagers assembled to hear the course and result of the debate. Perhaps in a similar manner the military and naval incidents, the contentions of mighty chiefs, the debates before the tent of Agamemnon, or in the council-house of Troy, were thrown into verse by the Father of poetry, the Prince of story-tellers, or, if the reader holds to the Wolfian theory, by the professional rhapsodists, and thus made known throughout Greece in the form of the Iliad. At any rate we have, in the practice still living in Serbia, an instance of the way in which a Serbian Homer would naturally have communicated to his countrymen all the details of meetings at the council-board and skirmishes in the plain which diversified the history of a siege, in the varying fortunes of which their interest was enlisted.

W. Denton.

THE BEAR'S SON.

ONCE upon a time a bear married a woman, and they had one son. When the boy was yet a little fellow he begged very hard to be allowed to leave the bear's cave, and to go out into the world to see what was in it. His father, however, the Bear, would not consent to this, saying, 'You are too young yet, and not strong enough. In the world there are multitudes of wicked beasts, called men, who will kill you.' So the boy was quieted for a while, and remained in the cave.

But, after some time, the boy prayed so earnestly that the Bear, his father, would let him go into the world, that the Bear brought him into the wood, and showed him a beech-tree, saying, 'If you can pull up that beech by the roots, I will let you go; but if you cannot, then this is a proof that you are still too weak, and must remain with me.' The boy tried to pull up the tree, but, after long trying, had to give it up, and go home again to the cave.

Again some time passed, and he then begged again to be allowed to go into the world, and his father told him, as before, if he could pull up the beech-tree he might go out into the world. This time the boy pulled up the tree, so the Bear consented to let him go, first, however, making him cut away the branches from the beech, so that he might use the trunk for a club. The boy now started on his journey, carrying the trunk of the beech over his shoulder.

One day as the Bear's son was journeying, he came to a field where he found hundreds of ploughmen working for their master. He asked them to give him something to eat, and they told him to wait a bit till their dinner was brought them, when he should have some —for, they said, 'Where so many are dining one mouth more or less matters but little.' Whilst they were speaking there came carts, horses, mules, and asses, all carrying the dinner. But when the meats were spread out the Bear's son declared he could eat all that up himself. The workmen wondered greatly at his words, not believing it possible that one man could consume as great a quantity of victuals as would satisfy several hundred men. This, however, the Bear's son persisted in affirming he could do, and offered to bet with them that he would do this. He proposed that the stakes should be all the iron of their ploughshares and other agricultural implements. To this they assented. No sooner had they made the wager than he fell upon the provisions, and in a short time consumed the whole. Not a fragment was left. Hereupon the labourers, in accordance with their wager, gave him all the iron which they possessed.

When the Bear's son had collected all the iron, he

tore up a young birch-tree, twisted it into a band and tied up the iron into a bundle, which he hung at the end of his staff, and throwing it across his shoulder, trudged off from the astonished and affrighted labourers.

Going on a short distance, he arrived at a forge in which a smith was employed making a ploughshare. This man he requested to make him a mace with the iron which he was carrying. This the smith undertook to do; but putting aside half the iron, he made of the rest a small, coarsely-finished mace.

Bear's son saw at a glance that he had been cheated by the smith. Moreover, he was disgusted at the roughness of the workmanship. He however took it, and declared his intention of testing it. Then fastening it to the end of his club and throwing it into the air high above the clouds he stood still and allowed it to fall on his shoulder. It had no sooner struck him than the mace shivered into fragments, some of which fell on and destroyed the forge. Taking up his staff, Bear's son reproached the smith for his dishonesty, and killed him on the spot.

Having collected the whole of the iron, the Bear's son went to another smithy, and desired the smith whom he found there to make him a mace, saying to him, 'Please play no tricks on me. I bring you these fragments of iron for you to use in making a mace. Beware that you do not attempt to cheat me as I was cheated before!' As the smith had heard what had happened to the other one, he collected his workpeople, threw all the iron on his fire, and welded the whole together and made a large mace of perfect workmanship.

When it was fastened on the head of his club the Bear's son, to prove it, threw it up high, and caught it on his back. This time the mace did not break, but rebounded. Then the Bear's son got up and said, 'This work is well done!' and, putting it on his shoulder, walked away. A little farther on he came to a field wherein a man was ploughing with two oxen, and he went up to him and asked for something to eat. The man said, 'I expect every moment my daughter to come with my dinner, then we shall see what God has given us!' The Bear's son told him how he had eaten up all the dinner prepared for many hundreds of ploughmen, and asked, 'From a dinner prepared for one person how much can come to me or to you?' Meanwhile the girl brought the dinner. The moment she put it down, Bear's son stretched out his hand to begin to eat, but the man stopped him. 'No!' said he, 'you must first say grace, as I do!' The Bear's son, hungry as he was, obeyed, and, having said grace, they both began to eat. The Bear's son, looking at the girl who brought the dinner (she was a tall, strong, beautiful girl), became very fond of her, and said to the father, 'Will you give me your daughter for a wife?' The man answered, 'I would give her to you very gladly but I have promised her already to the Moustached.' The Bear's son exclaimed, 'What do I care for Moustachio? I have my mace for him!' But the man answered, 'Hush! hush! Moustachio is also somebody! You will see him here soon.' Shortly after a noise was heard afar off, and lo! behind a hill a moustache showed itself, and in it were three hundred and sixty-five birds' nests. Shortly after appeared the other moustache, and then came Moustachio himself. Having reached them, he lay down on the ground immediately, to rest. He put his head on the girl's knee and told her to scratch his head a little. The girl obeyed him, and the Bear's son, getting up, struck him with his club over the head. Whereupon Moustachio, pointing to the place with his finger, said, 'Something bit me here!' The Bear's son struck with his mace on another spot, and Moustachio again pointed to the place, saying to the girl, 'Something has bitten me here!' When he was struck a third time, he said to the girl angrily, 'Look you! something bites me here!' Then the girl said, 'Nothing has bitten you; a man struck you!'

When Moustachio heard that he jumped up, but Bear's son had thrown away his mace and ran away. Moustachio pursued him, and though the Bear's son was lighter than he, and had gotten the start of him a considerable distance, he would not give up pursuing him.

At length the Bear's son, in the course of his flight, came to a wide river, and found, near it, some men threshing corn. 'Help me, my brothers, help—for God's sake!' he cried; 'help! Moustachio is pursuing me! What shall I do? How can I get across the river?' One of the men stretched out his shovel, saying, 'Here! sit down on it, and I will throw

c

you over the river!' The Bear's son sat on the shovel, and the man threw him over the water to the other shore. Soon after Moustachio came up, and asked, 'Has any one passed here?' The threshers replied that a man had passed. Moustachio demanded, 'How did he cross the river?' They answered, 'He sprang over.' Then Moustachio went back a little to take a start, and with a hop he sprang to the other side, and continued to pursue the Bear's son. Meanwhile this last, running hastily up a hill, got very tired. At the top of the hill he found a man sowing, and the sack with seeds was hanging on his neck. After every handful of seed sown in the ground, the man put a handful in his mouth and eat them. The Bear's son shouted to him, 'Help, brother, help!—for God's sake! Moustachio is following me, and will soon catch me! Hide me somewhere!' Then the man said, 'Indeed, it is no joke to have Moustachio pursuing you. But I have nowhere to hide you, unless in this sack among the seeds.' So he put him in the sack. When Moustachio came up to the sower he asked him if he had seen the Bear's son anywhere? The man replied, 'Yes, he passed by long ago, and God knows where he has got before this!'

Then Moustachio went back again. By-and-by the sower forgot that Bear's son was in his sack, and he took him out with a handful of seeds, and put him in his mouth. Then Bear's son was afraid of being swallowed, so he looked round the mouth quickly, and, seeing a hollow tooth, hid himself in it.

When the sower returned home in the evening, he

called to his sisters-in-law, 'Children, give me my toothpick! There is something in my broken tooth.' The sisters-in-law brought him two iron picks, and, standing one on each side, they poked about with the two picks in his tooth till the Bear's son jumped out. Then the man remembered him, and said, 'What bad luck you have! I had nearly swallowed you.'

After they had taken supper they talked about many different things, till at last the Bear's son asked what had happened to break that one tooth, whilst the others were all strong and healthy. Then the man told me in these words: 'Once upon a time ten of us started with thirty horses to the sea-shore to buy some salt. We found a girl in a field watching sheep, and she asked us where we were going. We said we were going to the sea-shore to buy salt. She said, 'Why go so far? I have in the bag in my hand here some salt which remained over after feeding the sheep. I think it will be enough for you.' So we settled about the price, and then she took the salt from her bag, whilst we took the sacks from the thirty horses, and we weighed the salt and filled the sacks with it till all the thirty sacks were full. We then paid the girl, and returned home. It was a very fine autumn day but as we were crossing a high mountain, the sky became very cloudy and it began to snow, and there was a cold north wind, so that we could not see our path and wandered about here and there. At last, by good luck, one of us shouted, 'Here, brothers! Here is a dry place!' So we went in one after the other till we were all, with the thirty horses, under shelter. Then we took the sacks from the horses, made a good fire, and passed the night there as if it were a house. Next morning, just think what we saw! We were all in one man's head, which lay in the midst of some vineyards; and whilst we were yet wondering and loading our horses, the keeper of the vineyards came and picked the head up. He put it in a sling and slinging it about several times, threw it over his head, and cast it far away over the vines to frighten the starlings away from his grapes. So we rolled down a hill, and it was then that I broke my tooth.'

THE WONDERFUL KIOSK.

ONCE upon a time there lived a king, who had three sons and one daughter. The daughter was kept by her father for safety in a cage, since he cared for her as for his own eyes. When the girl grew up, she one evening asked her father to let her walk a little with her brothers in the front of the palace, and her father granted her request. She had hardly, however, taken a step outside the door of the palace before a dragon came down, caught her away from her brothers, and flew up with her into the clouds.

The three brothers ran as quickly as they could, and told their father what had happened to their sister, and asked him to let them go in search of her. To this their father consented, and gave each of them a horse, and other needful things for their travelling, and they went away to find their sister. After they had travelled a long time, they came in sight of a kiosk, which was neither in the sky nor yet on the earth, but hung midway between both. On coming near it, they began to think that their sister might be in it, and they consulted together how they might contrive to reach it. After much deliberation they settled that one of them should kill his horse, make a thong out of the hide, and fastening one end of the thong to an arrow, shoot it from the bow so that it should strike deep in the side of the kiosk, and that thus they might be able to climb up to it. The youngest brother proposed to the eldest that he should kill his horse, but this he refused to do. In like manner the second brother refused, so that nothing remained but that the youngest should kill his horse, which he did and made a long thong out of the hide; to this he tied an arrow, which he shot towards the kiosk.

The question was then asked, who would climb up the thong? The eldest brother declared that he would not; the second also refused, and thus it was the youngest was forced to climb up. When he had reached the kiosk he went from room to room, until at length he found his sister sitting with the dragon sleeping with his head upon her knee, while she passed her fingers through the hair of his head.

When she saw her brother she was very much frightened, and made signs for him to go away before the dragon woke up. But this her brother would not do, and instead of going away took his mace and struck with all his might on the head of the dragon. The dragon moved his paw a little towards the place where he had been struck, and said to the maiden, 'I felt something bite me just here.' As he spoke the king's son gave him another blow, and the dragon said again, 'I felt something bite me just here.' When the brother lifted his mace to strike the third time, the sister pointed and showed him where to strike at the life of the dragon. So he struck at the life, and the dragon immediately fell down dead, and the king's daughter pushed him from her knee and ran quickly to her brother and kissed him. Then she took him by the hand and began to show him the various rooms of the kiosk.

First, she took him into a room where a black horse stood ready to be mounted, with all his riding-gear on him, and the whole of the harness was of pure silver.

She then led him to a second room, and in it stood a white horse, also saddled and bridled, and his harness was entirely of pure gold.

At last the sister took her brother into a third room, and there stood a cream-coloured horse, and the reins and stirrups and saddle, which were on him, were all thickly studded with precious stones.

After passing through these three rooms, she led him to a room where a young maiden sat behind a golden tambourette, busily engaged in embroidering with golden thread.

From this room they went into another, where a girl was spinning gold thread, and again into another room where a girl sat threading pearls, and before her, on a golden plate, was a golden hen with her chickens, sorting the pearls.

Having seen all these things, the brother went back to the room where the dragon lay dead, and threw him down to the earth, and the two brothers, who were below, were almost frightened to death at the sight of the dragon's carcass. The young prince then let his sister slowly down, and, after her, the three young maidens, each of them with the work on which she was employed. As he let them down, one after the other, he shouted to his brothers and told them to whom each of the maidens should belong—reserving for himself the third one, whom he also let down to the ground. This was the maiden who was engaged in threading pearls with the help of the golden hen and chickens. His brothers, however, were envious at the success of his courage, and at his having found his sister and saved her from the dragon, so they cut the thong in order that he might not be able to get down from the kiosk.

Then they found, in the fields near, a young shepherd, whom they disguised and took to their father, but forbad their sister and the three maidens, with many threats, to tell what they had done. After some time the youngest brother, who had been left in the kiosk, received the news that his two brothers and the shepherd were to marry the three maidens. On the day when his eldest brother was married, the youngest brother mounted his black horse, and just as the wedding party came back from the church, the young prince came down from the kiosk, rushed into the midst, and struck his eldest brother slightly in the back, so that he fell down from his horse; he then immediately flew back again to the kiosk. On the day that his second brother was married, the youngest again came down among the wedding party, as they left the church. He was mounted on the white horse, and he struck his second brother as he had done the eldest, so that he also fell down, and then he returned again to the kiosk. At last, on hearing that the young shepherd was going to be married to the maiden whom the prince had selected for himself, he mounted on the cream-coloured horse, descended again, and rode among the wedding guests as they came out of the church, and struck the bridegroom with his mace on his head so that he at once fell down dead. When the guests gathered round him to catch him, which he permitted them to do, making no attempt to escape from them, he soon proved to them that he himself was the third son of the king, and that the shepherd was an imposter, and that his brothers, out of envy, had left him in the kiosk, when he had found his sister and killed the dragon. His sister and the three young maidens confirmed all that he said, so that the king, in his anger at the two elder brothers, drove them away from his court; however, he married the youngest brother to the third maiden, and, at his death, left him his kingdom.

THE SNAKE'S GIFT. LANGUAGE OF ANIMALS.

ONCE upon a time there lived a shepherd who served his master faithfully and honestly. One day, whilst keeping the sheep in the forest, he heard a hissing, and wondered what the noise could be. So he went farther into the wood to try and find out. There he saw that the forest was on fire, and a snake was hissing in the midst of the flames. The shepherd watched to see what the snake would do, for it was quite surrounded by the fire, which approached it nearer and nearer. Then the snake cried out, 'For God's sake, good shepherd, save me from the fire!' So the shepherd stretched his crook across the flames and the snake glided rapidly over the staff and up his arm on to his shoulder, till at last it wound itself round his neck. Then the shepherd was terrified and exclaimed, 'What shall I do? What an unlucky wretch I am! I saved you, and now you are about to kill me!' The snake answered, 'Do not be afraid; only take me to the house of my father. My father is the king of snakes.' But the shepherd, being already in great fear, began to excuse himself, saying he must not leave his sheep. Then the snake said, 'Nothing will happen to your sheep. Do not be anxious about them. But let us hurry home.'

So the shepherd went on with the snake through the forest, until they came to a gate made entirely of snakes. Then the snake on the neck of the shepherd hissed, and instantly the snakes untwined themselves, so that the man could pass through. As soon as they had gone through, the snake said to him, 'When you reach my father's house he will offer to give you whatever you like—gold, silver, or precious stones. Do not, however, take any of these things. Choose, instead, the language of animals. He will hesitate at first, but at last he will give it you.' Meanwhile they arrived at the palace, and the king of snakes said, weeping, 'For God's sake, my child, where were you?' Thereupon the snake told him all that had happened, how he had been surrounded by fire, and how the shepherd had saved him. Then the snake king said to the shepherd, 'What do you wish that I should give you for saving my son?'

The shepherd answered, 'I desire nothing but the language of animals.' The snake king, however, said, 'That is not good for you, for if I give it you, and you tell any one about it, you will instantly die. Therefore it is better that you ask me for something else.' 'If you wish to give me anything,' replied the shepherd, 'give me the language of animals; if you will not give me that, I want nothing—so good-bye,' and he turned to go away. Then the snake king called him back, saying, 'If you indeed wish it so much, take it. Open your mouth.' The shepherd did so, and the snake king blew into his mouth and said, 'Now blow once yourself in my mouth.' The shepherd did so, and then the snake king blew again into his mouth, and this they did three times. After that the snake said, 'Now, you possess the language of animals; go, in God's name, but do not for the world tell any one about it. If you tell any one you will instantly die.'

The shepherd returned across the forest, and, passing through it, he understood everything the birds and animals, and even the plants, were saying to each other. When he came to his sheep he found them all there, safe and sound, so he laid himself down to rest a little. Hardly had he done so before two or three ravens settled on a tree near him, and began to converse together, saying, 'If that shepherd only knew that just on the spot where the black sheep is lying there is, deep in the earth, a cave full of gold and silver!' When the shepherd heard that he went off to his master and told him. The master brought a cart, and dug down to the cave, and carried the treasure away home. But the master was honest, so he gave up the whole of the treasure to the shepherd, saying, 'Here my son, all this wealth belongs to you. For to you God gave it. Build a house, marry, and live upon the treasure.' So the shepherd took the money, built a house, and married, and by-and-by he became the richest man in the whole neighbourhood. He kept his own shepherd, and cattle-driver, and swineherd; in short, he had great property and made much money.

Once, just at Christmas, he said to his wife, 'Get ready some wine and other food, and to-morrow we will feast the shepherds.' The wife did so, and in the morning they went to their farm. Towards evening the master said to the shepherds, 'Come here, all of you; you shall eat, drink, and make merry together, and I will go myself this night to watch the sheep.'

So the master went to watch his sheep, and, about midnight, the wolves began to howl and the dogs to bark. The wolves spoke, in wolf language, 'May we come and take something? You, also, shall get a part of the prey.' And the dogs answered, in dog language, 'Come! we also are ready to eat something.' But there was one old dog there who had only two teeth left. This old dog shouted furiously, 'Come on, you miserable wretches, if you dare. So long as I have these two teeth left you shall not do any damage to my master's property.' All this the master heard and understood. Next day he ordered all the dogs to be killed except that old one. The servants began to remonstrate, saying, 'For God's sake, master, it is a pity to do this.' But the master answered, 'Do as I have ordered you,' and started with his wife to go home. They rode on horseback, he on a fine horse and his wife on a handsome mare. But the master's horse went so fast that the wife remained a little behind. Then the master's horse neighed, and said to the mare, 'Come on, why do you stay behind?' And the mare answered, 'Ah, to you it is easy—you are carrying only one weight, and I am carrying three.' Thereupon the man turned his head and laughed. The wife saw him laughing, and urged the mare on quicker till she came up to her husband, and asked him, 'Why were you laughing?' He said merely, 'I had good reason to laugh!' But the wife was not satisfied, and again begged he would tell her why he laughed. He excused himself, exclaiming, 'Give up questioning me; what has come to you, my wife? I forget now why it was I laughed.' But the more he refused to tell her, the more she wished to know. At last the man said, 'If I tell you I shall die immediately!' That, however, did not quiet her, and she kept on asking, saying to him, 'You must tell me.' In the meantime they reached their house. When they had done so the man ordered a coffin to be made, and, when it was ready, had it placed in front of the house, and laid himself down in it. Then he said to his wife, 'Now I will tell you why I laughed, but the moment I tell you I shall die.' So he looked around once more, and saw that the old dog had come from the field, and had taken his stand over his head, and was howling. When the man noticed this he said to his wife, 'Bring a piece of bread for this poor dog.' The wife brought a piece and threw it to the dog, but the dog did not even look at it, and a cock came near and began to peck at it.

Then the dog said to the cock, 'You think only about

eating. Do you know that our master is going to die?' And the cock answered, 'Well, let him die, since he is such a fool. I have a hundred wives, and often at nights I gather them all round a grain of corn, and, when they are all there, I pick it up myself. If any of them are angry, I peck them; that is my way of keeping them quiet. Only look at the master, however; he is not able to rule one single wife!'

The man, hearing that, got out of the coffin, took a stick, and called his wife to him, saying, 'Come now, and I will tell you what you want to know.' The wife, seeing she was in danger of getting a beating, left him in peace, and never asked him again why it was he laughed.

THE GOLDEN APPLE-TREE, AND THE NINE PEAHENS.

ONCE upon a time there lived a king who had three sons. Now, before the king's palace grew a golden apple-tree, which in one and the same night blossomed, bore fruit, and lost all its fruit, though no one could tell who took the apples. One day the king, speaking to his eldest son, said, 'I should like to know who takes the fruit from our apple-tree!' And the son said, 'I will keep guard to-night, and will see who gathers the apples.' So when the evening came he went and laid himself down, under the apple-tree, upon the ground to watch. Just, however, as the apples ripened, he fell asleep, and when he awoke in the morning, there was not a single one left on the tree. Whereupon he went and told his father what had happened. Then the second son offered to keep watch by the tree, but he had no better success than his eldest brother.

So the turn came to the king's youngest son to keep guard. He made his preparations, brought his bed under the tree, and immediately went to sleep. Before midnight he awoke and looked up at the tree, and saw how the apples ripened, and how the whole palace was lit up by their shining. At that minute nine peahens flew towards the tree, and eight of them settled on its branches, but the ninth alighted near him and turned instantly into a beautiful girl—so beautiful, indeed, that the whole kingdom could not produce one who could in any way compare with her. She stayed, conversing kindly with him, till after midnight, then thanking him for the golden apples, she prepared to depart; but, as he begged she would leave him one, she gave him two, one for himself and one for the king his father. Then the girl turned again into a peahen, and flew away with the other eight. Next morning, the king's son took the two apples to his father, and the king was much pleased, and praised his son. When the evening came, the king's youngest son took his place again under the apple-tree to keep guard over it. He again conversed as he had done the night before with the beautiful girl, and brought to his father, the next morning, two apples as before. But, after he had succeeded so well several nights, his two elder brothers grew envious because he had been able to do what they could not. At length they found an old woman, who promised to discover how the youngest brother had succeeded in saving the two apples. So, as the evening came, the old woman stole softly under the bed which stood under the apple-tree, and hid herself. And after a while, came also the king's son, and laid himself down as usual to sleep. When it was near midnight the nine peahens flew up as before, and eight of them settled on the branches, and the ninth stood by his bed, and turned into a most beautiful girl.

Then the old woman slowly took hold of one of the girl's curls, and cut it off, and the girl immediately rose up, changed again into a peahen and flew away, and the other peahens followed her, and so they all disappeared. Then the king's son jumped up, and cried out, 'What is that?' and, looking under the bed, he saw the old woman, and drew her out. Next morning he ordered her to be tied to a horse's tail, and so torn to pieces. But the peahens never came back, so the king's son was very sad for a long time, and wept at his loss. At length he resolved to go and look after his peahen, and never to come back again unless he should find her. When he told the king his father of his intention, the king begged him not to go away, and said that he would find him another beautiful girl, and that he might choose out of the whole kingdom.

But all the king's persuasions were useless. His son went into the world to search everywhere for his peahen, taking only one servant to serve him. After many travels he came one day to a lake. Now by the lake stood a large and beautiful palace. In the palace lived an old woman as queen, and with the queen lived a girl, her daughter. He said to the old woman, 'For heaven's sake, grandmother, do you know anything about nine golden peahens?' and the old woman answered, 'Oh, my son, I know all about them; they come every mid-day to bathe in the lake. But what do you want with them? Let them be, think nothing about them. Here is my daughter. Such a beautiful girl! and such a heiress! All my wealth will remain to you if you marry her.' But he, burning with desire to see the peahens, would not listen to what the old woman spoke about her daughter.

Next morning, when day dawned, the prince prepared to go down to the lake to wait for the peahens. Then the old queen bribed the servant and gave him a little pair of bellows, and said, 'Do you see these bellows? When you come to the lake you must blow secretly with them behind his neck, and then he will fall asleep, and not be able to speak to the peahens.' The mischievous servant did as the old woman told him; when he went with his master down to the lake, he took occasion to blow with the bellows behind his neck, and the poor prince fell asleep just as though he were dead. Shortly after, the nine peahens came flying, and eight of them alighted by the lake, but the ninth flew towards him, as he sat on horseback, and caressed him, and tried to awaken him. 'Awake, my darling! 'Awake, my heart! Awake, my soul!' But for all that he knew nothing, just as if he were dead. After they had bathed, all the peahens flew away together, and after they were gone the prince woke up, and said to his servant, 'What has happened? Did they not come?' The servant told him they had been there, and that eight of them had bathed, but the ninth had sat by him on his horse, and caressed and tried to awaken him. Then the king's son was so angry that he almost killed himself in his rage. Next morning he went down again to the shore to wait for the peahens, and rode about a long time till the servant again found an opportunity of blowing with the bellows behind his neck, so that he again fell asleep as though dead. Hardly had he fallen asleep when the nine peahens came flying, and eight of them alighted by the water, but the ninth settled down by the side of his horse and caressed him, and cried out to awaken him, 'Arise, my darling! Arise, my heart! Arise, my soul!'

But it was of no use; the prince slept on as if he were dead. Then she said to the servant, 'Tell your master to-morrow he can see us here again, but never more.' With these words the peahens flew away. Immediately after the king's son woke up, and asked his servant, 'Have they not been here?' And the man answered, 'Yes, they have been, and say that you can see them again to-morrow, at this place, but after that they will not return again.' When the unhappy prince heard that, he knew not what to do with himself, and in his great trouble and misery tore the hair from his head.

The third day he went down again to the shore, but, fearing to fall asleep, instead of riding slowly, galloped along the shore. His servant, however, found an opportunity of blowing with the bellows behind his neck, and again the prince fell asleep. A moment after came the nine peahens, and the eight alighted on the lake and the ninth by him, on his horse, and sought to awaken him, caressing him. 'Arise, my darling!

Arise, my heart! Arise, my soul!' But it was of no use, he slept on as if dead. Then the peahen said to the servant, 'When your master awakens tell him he ought to strike off the head of the nail from the lower part, and then he will find me.' Thereupon all the peahens fled away. Immediately the king's son awoke, and said to his servant, 'Have they been here?' And the servant answered, 'They have been, and the one which alighted on your horse, ordered me to tell you to strike off the head of the nail from the lower part, and then you will find her.' When the prince heard that, he drew his sword and cut off his servant's head.

After that he travelled alone about the world, and, after long travelling, came to a mountain and remained all night there with a hermit, whom he asked if he knew anything about nine golden peahens. The hermit said, 'Eh! my son, you are lucky; God has led you in the right path. From this place it is only half a day's walk. But you must go straight on, then you will come to a large gate, which you must pass through; and, after that, you must keep always to the right hand, and so you will come to the peahens' city, and there find their palace.' So next morning the king's son arose, and prepared to go. He thanked the hermit, and went as he had told him. After a while he came to the great gate, and, having passed it, turned to the right, so that at mid-day he saw the city, and beholding how white it shone, rejoiced very much. When he came into the city he found the palace where lived the nine golden peahens. But at the gate he was stopped by the guard, who demanded who he was, and whence he came. After he had answered these questions, the guards went to announce him to the queen. When the queen heard who he was, she came running out to the gate and took him by the hand to lead him into the palace. She was a young and beautiful maiden, and so there was a great rejoicing when, after a few days, he married her and remained there with her.

One day, some time after their marriage, the queen went out to walk, and the king's son remained in the palace. Before going out, however, the queen gave him the keys of twelve cellars, telling him, 'You may go down into all the cellars except the twelfth—that you must on no account open, or it will cost you your head.' She then went away. The king's son whilst remaining in the palace began to wonder what there could be in the twelfth cellar, and soon commenced opening one cellar after the other. When he came to the twelfth he would not at first open it, but again began to wonder very much why he was forbidden to go into it. 'What *can* be in this cellar?' he exclaimed to himself. At last he opened it. In the middle of the cellar lay a big barrel with an open bunghole, but bound fast round with three iron hoops. Out of the barrel came a voice, saying, 'For God's sake, my brother—I am dying with thirst—please give me a cup of water!' Then the king's son took a cup and filled it with water, and emptied it into the barrel. Immediately he had done so one of the hoops burst asunder. Again came the voice from the barrel, 'For

THE GOLDEN APPLE-TREE.   49

God's sake, my brother—I am dying of thirst—please give me a cup of water!' The king's son again filled the cup, and took it, and emptied it into the barrel, and instantly another hoop burst asunder. The third time the voice came out of the barrel, 'For God's sake, my brother—I am dying of thirst—please give me a cup of water!' The king's son again took the cup and filled it, and poured the water into the barrel—and the third hoop burst. Then the barrel fell to pieces, and a dragon flew out of the cellar, and caught the queen on the road and carried her away.

Then the servant, who went out with the queen, came back quickly, and told the king's son what had happened, and the poor prince knew not what to do with himself, so desperate was he, and full of self-reproaches. At length, however, he resolved to set out and travel through the world in search of her. After long journeying, one day he came to a lake, and near it, in a little hole, he saw a little fish jumping about. When the fish saw the king's son, she began to beg pitifully, 'For God's sake, be my brother, and throw me into the water. Some day I may be of use to you, so take now a little scale from me, and when you need me, rub it gently.' Then the king's son lifted the little fish from the hole and threw her into the water, after he had taken one small scale, which he wrapped up carefully in a handkerchief. Some time afterwards, as he travelled about the world, he came upon a fox, caught in an iron trap. When the fox saw the prince, he spoke: 'In God's name, be a brother to me, and help me to get out of this trap. One day you will need me, so take just one hair from my tail, and when you want me, rub it gently.' Then the king's son took a hair from the tail of the fox, and let him free.

Again, as he crossed a mountain, he found a wolf fast in a trap; and when the wolf saw him, it spoke: 'Be a brother to me; in God's name, set me free, and one day I will help you. Only take a hair from me, and when you need me, rub it gently.' So he took a hair, and let the wolf free. After that, the king's son travelled about a very long time, till one day he met a man, to whom he said, 'For God's sake, brother, have you ever heard any one say where is the palace of the dragon king?' The man gave him very particular directions which way to take, and in what length of time he could get there. Then the king's son thanked him and continued his journey until he came to the city where the dragon lived. When there, he went into the palace and found therein his wife, and both of them were exceedingly pleased to meet each other, and began to take counsel how they could escape. They resolved to run away, and prepared hastily for the journey. When all was ready they mounted on horseback and galloped away. As soon as they were gone the dragon came home, also on horseback, and, entering his palace, found that the queen had gone away. Then he said to his horse, 'What shall we do now? Shall we eat and drink, or go at once after them?' The horse answered, 'Let us eat and drink first, we shall anyway catch them; do not be anxious.'

After the dragon had dined he mounted his horse, and in a few moments came up with the runaways. Then he took the queen from the king's son and said to him, 'Go now, in God's name! This time I forgive you because you gave me water in the cellar; but if your life is dear to you do not come back here any more!' The unhappy young prince went on his way a little, but could not long resist, so he came back next day to the dragon's palace, and found the queen sitting alone and weeping. Then they began again to consult how they could get away. And the prince said, 'When the dragon comes, ask him where he got that horse, and then you will tell me so that I can look for such another one; perhaps in this way we can escape.' He then went away, lest the dragon should come and find him with the queen.

By-and-by the dragon came home, and the queen began to pet him, and speak lovingly to him about many things, till at last she said, 'Ah! what a fine horse you have! where did you get such a splendid horse?' And he answered, 'Eh! where I got it every one cannot get one! In such and such a mountain lives an old woman who has twelve horses in her stable, and no one can say which is the finest, they are all so beautiful. But in one corner of the stable stands a horse which looks as if he were leprous, but, in truth, he is the very best horse in the whole world. He is the brother of my horse, and whoever gets him may ride to the sky. But whoever wishes to get a horse from that old woman, must serve her three days and three nights. She has a mare with a foal, and whoever during three nights guards and keeps for her this mare and this foal, has a right to claim the best horse from the old woman's stable. But whoever engages to keep watch over the mare and does not, must lose his head!'

Next day, when the dragon went out, the king's son came, and the queen told him all she had learned from the dragon. Then the king's son went away to the mountain and found the old woman, and entered her house greeting: 'God help you, grandmother!' And she answered, 'God help you, too, my son! what do you wish?' 'I should like to serve you,' said the king's son. Then the old woman said, 'Well, my son, if you keep my mare safe for three days and three nights I will give you the best horse, and you can choose him yourself; but if you do not keep the mare safe you shall lose your head.'

Then she led him into the courtyard, where all around stakes were ranged. Each of them had on it a man's head, except one stake, which had no head on it, and shouted incessantly, "Oh, grandmother, give me a head!" The old woman showed all this to the prince, and said, 'Look here! all these were heads of those who tried to keep my mare, and they have lost their heads for their pains!'

But the prince was not a bit afraid, so he stayed to serve the old woman. When the evening came he mounted the mare and rode her into the field, and the foal followed. He sat still on her back, having made up his mind not to dismount, that he might be sure of her. But before midnight he slumbered a little, and when he awoke he found himself sitting on a rail and holding the bridle in his hand. Then he was greatly alarmed, and went instantly to look about to find the mare, and whilst looking for her, he came to a piece of water. When he saw the water he remembered the little fish, and took the scale from the handkerchief and rubbed it a little. Then immediately the little fish appeared and said, 'What is the matter, my half-brother?' And he replied, 'The mare of the old woman ran away whilst under my charge, and now I do not know where she is!' And the fish answered, 'Here she is, turned to a fish, and the foal to a smaller one. But strike once upon the water with the bridle and cry out, "Heigh! mare of the old woman!"' The prince did as he was told, and immediately the mare came, with the foal, out of the water to the shore. Then he put on her the bridle and mounted and rode away to the old woman's house, and the foal followed. When he got there the old woman gave him his breakfast; she, however, took the mare into the stable and beat her with a poker, saying, 'Why did you not go down among the fishes, you cursed mare?' And the mare answered, 'I have been down to the fishes, but the fish are his friends and they told him about me.' Then the old woman said, 'Then go among the foxes!'

When evening came the king's son mounted the mare and rode to the field, and the foal followed the mare. Again he sat on the mare's back until near midnight, when he fell asleep as before. When he awoke, he found himself riding on the rail and holding the bridle in his hand. So he was much frightened, and went to look after the mare. As he went he remembered the words the old woman had said to the mare, and he took from the handkerchief the fox's hair and rubbed it a little between his fingers. All at once the fox stood before him, and asked, 'What is the matter, half-brother?' And he said, 'The old woman's mare has run away, and I do not know where she can be.' Then the fox answered, 'Here she is with us; she has turned into a fox, and the foal into a cub; but strike once with the bridle on the earth and cry out, "Heigh! you old woman's mare!"' So the king's son struck with the bridle on the earth and cried, 'Heigh! old woman's mare!' and the mare came and stood, with her foal, near him. He put on the bridle, and mounted and rode off home, and the foal followed the mare. When he arrived the old woman gave him his breakfast, but took the mare into the stable and beat her with the poker, crying, 'To the foxes, cursed one! to the foxes!' And the mare answered, 'I have been with the foxes, but they are his friends, and told him I was there!' Then the old woman cried, 'If that is so, you must go among the wolves!'

When it grew dark again the king's son mounted the mare and rode out to the field, and the foal galloped by the side of the mare. Again he sat still on the mare's back till about midnight, when he grew very sleepy and fell into a slumber, as on the former evenings, and when he awoke he found himself riding on the rail.

holding the bridle in his hand, just as before. Then, as before, he went in a hurry to look after the mare. As he went he remembered the words the old woman had said to the mare, and took the wolf's hair from the handkerchief and rubbed it a little. Then the wolf came up to him and asked, 'What is the matter, half-brother?' And he answered, 'The old woman's mare has run away, and I cannot tell where she is.' The wolf said, 'Here she is with us; she has turned herself into a wolf, and the foal into a wolf's cub. Strike once with the bridle on the earth and cry out, "Heigh! old woman's mare!"' And the king's son did so, and instantly the mare came again and stood with the foal beside him. So he bridled her, and galloped home, and the foal followed. When he arrived the old woman gave him his breakfast, but she led the mare into the stable and beat her with the poker, crying, 'To the wolves, I said, miserable one!' Then the mare answered, 'I have been to the wolves; but they are his friends, and told him all about me!' Then the old woman came out of the stable, and the king's son said to her, 'Eh! grandmother, I have served you honestly; now give me what you promised me.' And the old woman answered, 'My son, what is promised must be fulfilled. So look here: here are the twelve horses, choose which you like!' And the prince said, 'Why should I be too particular? Give me only that leprous horse in the corner! fine horses are not fitting for me!' But the old woman tried to persuade him to choose another horse, saying, 'How can you be so foolish as to choose that leprous thing whilst there are such very fine horses here?' But he remained firm by his first choice, and said to the old woman, 'You ought to give me which I choose, for so you promised.' So, when the old woman found she could not make him change his mind, she gave him the scabby horse, and he took leave of her, and went away, leading the horse by the halter.

When he came to a forest he curried and rubbed down the horse, when it shone as bright as gold. He then mounted, and the horse flew as quickly as a bird, and in a few seconds brought him to the dragon's palace. The king's son went in and said to the queen, 'Get ready as soon as possible!' She was soon ready, when they both mounted the horse, and began their journey home. Soon after the dragon came home, and when he saw the queen had disappeared, said to his horse, 'What shall we do? Shall we eat and drink first, or shall we pursue them at once?' The horse answered, 'Whether we eat and drink or not it is all one, we shall never reach them.'

When the dragon heard that, he got quickly on his horse and galloped after them. When they saw the dragon following them they pushed on quicker, but their horse said, 'Do not be afraid! there is no need to run away.' In a very few moments the dragon came very near to them, and his horse said to their horse, 'For God's sake, my brother, wait a moment! I shall kill myself running after you!' Their horse answered, 'Why are you so stupid as to carry that monster.

Fling your heels up and throw him off, and come along with me!' When the dragon's horse heard that he shook his head angrily and flung his feet high in the air, so that the dragon fell off and brake in pieces, and his horse came up to them. Then the queen mounted him and returned with the king's son happily to her kingdom, where they reigned together in great prosperity until the day of their death.

PAPALLUGA;* OR, THE GOLDEN SLIPPER.

AS some village girls were spinning whilst they tended the cattle grazing in the neighbourhood of a ravine, an old man with a long white beard—so long a beard that it reached to his girdle—approached them, and said, 'Girls, girls, take care of that ravine! If one of you should drop her spindle down the cliff, her mother will be turned into a cow that very moment!'

Having warned them thus, the old man went away again. The girls, wondering very much at what he had told them, came nearer and nearer to the ravine, and leant over to look in; whilst doing so one of the girls—and she the most beautiful of them all—let her spindle fall from her hand, and it fell to the bottom of the ravine.

When she went home in the evening she found her mother, changed into a cow, standing before the house; and from that time forth she had to drive this cow to the pasture with the other cattle.

In a little time the father of the girl married a widow, who brought with her into the house her own

* Servian name for " Cinderella."

daughter. The stepmother immediately began to hate the step-daughter, because the girl was incomparably more beautiful than her own daughter. She forbade her to wash herself, to comb her hair, or to change her clothes, and sought by every possible way to torment and scold her. One day she gave her a bag full of hemp, and said, 'If you do not spin all this well and wind it, you need not return home, for if you do I shall kill you.'

The poor girl, walked behind the cattle and spun as fast as possible; but at mid-day, seeing how very little she had been able to spin, she began to weep. When the cow, her mother, saw her weeping, she asked her what was the matter, and the girl told her all about it. Then the cow consoled her, and told her not to be anxious. 'I will take the hemp in my mouth and chew it,' she said, 'and it will come out of my ear as thread, so that you can draw it out and wind it at once upon the stick;' and so it happened. The cow began to chew the hemp and the girl drew the thread from her ear and wound it, so that very soon they had quite finished the task.

When the girl went home in the evening, and took all the hemp, worked up, to her stepmother, she was greatly astonished, and next morning gave her yet more hemp to spin and wind. When at night she brought that home ready the stepmother thought she must be helped by some other girls, her friends; therefore the third day she gave her much more hemp than before. But when the girl had gone with the cow to the pasture, the woman sent her own daughter after her to find out who was helping her. This girl went quietly towards her step-sister so as not to be heard, and saw the cow chewing the hemp and the girl drawing the thread from her ear and winding it, so she hastened home and told all to her mother. Then the stepmother urged the husband to kill the cow. At first he resisted; but, seeing his wife would give him no peace, he at last consented to do as she wished, and fixed the day on which he would kill it. As soon as the step-daughter heard this she began to weep, and when the cow asked her why she wept she told her all about it. But the cow said, 'Be quiet! do not cry! Only when they kill me take care not to eat any of the meat, and be sure to gather all my bones and bury them behind the house, and whenever you need anything come to my grave and you will find help.' So when they killed the cow the girl refused to eat any of the flesh, saying she was not hungry, and afterwards carefully gathered all the bones and buried them behind the house, on the spot the cow had told her.

The real name of this girl was Mary, but as she had worked so much in the house, carrying water, cooking, washing dishes, sweeping the house, and doing all sorts of house-work, and had very much to do about the fire and cinders, her stepmother and half-sister called her 'Papalluga' (Cinderella).

One day the stepmother got ready to go with her own daughter to church, but before she went she spread over the house a basketful of millet, and said to her step-daughter, 'You Papalluga! If you do not gather up all this millet and get the dinner ready before we come back from church, I will kill you!'

When they had gone to church the poor girl began to weep, saying to herself: 'It is easy to see after the dinner; I shall soon have that ready; but who can gather up all this quantity of millet!' At that moment she remembered what the cow had told her, that in case of need she should go to her grave and would there find help, so she ran quickly to the spot, and what do you think she saw there? On the grave stood a large box full of valuable clothes of different kinds, and on the top of the box sat two white doves, who said, 'Mary, take out of this box the clothes which you like best and put them on, and then go to church; meanwhile we will pick up the millet seeds and put everything in order.' The girl was greatly pleased, and took the first clothes which came to hand. These were all of silk, and having put them on she went away to church. In the church every one, men and women, wondered much at her beauty and her splendid clothes, but no one knew who she was or whence she came. The king's son, who happened to be there, looked at her all the time and admired her greatly. Before the service was ended she stood up and quietly left the church. She then ran away home, and as soon as she got there took off her fine clothes and again laid them in the box, which instantly shut itself and disappeared.

Then she hurried to the hearth and found the dinner quite ready, all the millet gathered up, and everything in very good order. Soon after the stepmother came back with her daughter from the church, and was extremely surprised to find all the millet picked up and everything so well arranged.

Next Sunday the stepmother and her daughter again dressed themselves to go to church, and, before she went away, the stepmother threw much more millet about the floor, and said to her stepdaughter, 'If you do not gather up all this millet, prepare the dinner, and get everything into the best order, I shall kill you.' When they were gone, the girl instantly ran to her mother's grave, and there found the box open as before, with the two doves sitting on its lid. The doves said to her, 'Dress yourself, Mary, and go to church; we will pick up all the millet and arrange everything.' Then she took from the box silver clothes, and having dressed herself, went to church. In the church everyone, as before, admired her very much, and the king's son never moved his eyes from her. Just before the end of the service the girl again got up very quietly and stole through the crowd. When she got out of church she ran away very quickly, took off the clothes, laid them in the box, and went into the kitchen. When the stepmother and her daughter came home, they were more surprised than before; the millet was gathered up, dinner was ready, and everything in the very best order. They wondered very much how it was all done.

On the third Sunday the stepmother dressed herself to go with her daughter to church, and again scattered millet about on the ground, but this time far more than on the other Sundays. Before she went out she said to her step-daughter, 'If you do not gather up all this millet, prepare the dinner, and have everything in order when I come from church, I will kill you!' The instant they were gone, the girl ran to her mother's grave, and found the box open with the two white doves sitting on the lid. The doves told her to dress herself and go to church, and to have no care about the millet or dinner.

This time she took clothes of all real gold out of the box, and, having put them on, went away to the church. In the church all the people looked at her and admired her exceedingly. Now the king's son had resolved not to let her slip away as before, but to watch where she went. So, when the service was nearly ended, and she stood up to leave the church, the king's son followed her, but was not able to reach her. In pushing through the crowd, however, Mary somehow in her hurry lost the slipper from her right foot and had no time to look for it. This slipper the king's son found, and took care of it. When the girl got home she took off the golden clothes and laid them in the box, and went immediately to the fire in the kitchen.

The king's son, having determined to find the maiden, went all over the kingdom, and tried the slipper on every girl, but in some cases it was too long, in others too short, and, in fact, it did not fit any of them. As he was thus going about from one house to the other, the king's son came at last to the house of the girl's father, and the stepmother, seeing the king's son coming, hid her step-daughter in a wash-trough before the house. When the king's son came in with the slipper and asked if there were any girl in the house, the woman answered 'Yes,' and brought out her own daughter. But when the slipper was tried it was found it would not go even over the girl's toes. Then the king's son asked if no other girl was there, and the stepmother said, 'No, there is no other in the house.' At that moment the cock sprung upon the wash-trough, and crowed out 'Cock-a-doodle-do!—here she is under the wash-trough!

The stepmother shouted, 'Go away! may the eagle fly away with you!' But the king's son, hearing that, hurried to the wash-trough, and lifted it up, and what did he see there! The same girl who had been in the church, in the same golden clothes in which she had appeared the third time there, but lying under the trough, and with only one slipper on. When the king's son saw her, he nearly lost his senses for the moment, he was so very glad. Then he quickly tried to place the slipper he carried on her right foot, and it fitted her exactly, besides perfectly matching with the other slipper on her left foot. Then he took her away with him to his palace and married her.

THE GOLDEN-FLEECED RAM.

ONCE upon a time a hunter went to the mountains to hunt, and met there a golden-fleeced ram. The moment he saw it he took up his rifle to shoot it; before, however, he could do so, the ram rushed at him and killed him with its horns. His friends found him lying dead, and took him home and buried him, without knowing how he had been killed. The hunter's wife hung up his rifle on a nail. When her son grew old enough, he one day asked his mother for the rifle, that he might go hunting. The mother, however, refused to give it him. 'Nothing in the world, my son,' cried she, 'shall induce me to do so. Your father lost his life through that gun, and do you wish, also, to lose your life because of it?'

However the youth managed to steal the rifle one day, and went away to the mountains to hunt. When he came to the forest, the golden-fleeced ram appeared also to him, and said, 'I killed your father, and I will kill you!' The son was shocked, and said, 'God help me!' Then he levelled at the ram with the rifle and killed it.

Greatly rejoiced that he had killed the golden-fleeced ram, (for there was not another like it in all the kingdom) he now took the fleece home. In a very short time the news of this spread all over the country, and reached even the king's ears. Then the king ordered the young lad to bring the ram's fleece to him, that he might see what different animals lived in his kingdom. When the young lad took it to the king, and exhibited it, the king asked, 'How much money do you want for that fleece?' To which the young man answered, 'I will not sell it for any money.'

Now the king's first minister happened to be the uncle of the young man; instead, however, of being his friend, he was his greatest enemy.' So the minister said to the king, 'If he will not give you the fleece, set him something to do which will cost him his life. The best plan would be to order him to do something which it is impossible for him to do.' Accordingly he advised the king to order the young man to plant a vineyard, and to bring him, within seven days, new wine from it. The young man hearing this, began to weep, and begged to be excused from such a task as he could not work a miracle. But the king said, 'If you don't do that in seven days, you shall lose your life.'

Then the youth returned weeping to his mother, and told her about it. And the mother said, 'Did I not tell you, my son, that the golden fleece would cost you your life as it cost your father his?' Weeping and wondering what to do, since he got no rest at home, he thus walked out of the village a good distance, when, suddenly, a little girl appeared before him and said, 'Why are you weeping, my brother?' He answered, somewhat angrily, 'Go your way, in God's name! you cannot help me.' He then went on his way, but the little girl followed him, and begged much that he would tell her why he wept, 'for, perhaps,' said she, 'I may be able to help you.' 'Well, then, I will tell you,' said he, 'though I am sure no one except God can help me.' So he told her all that had happened to him, and what the king had ordered him to do. When she had heard all, she said, 'Be not tearful, my brother, but go and demand from the king that he should appoint the place where the vineyard shall be planted, and order it to be dug in straight lines; then go yourself, and take a sack, with a branch of basilicum in it, and lie down to sleep in the place where the vineyard has been marked out. Take courage! Don't be afraid! In seven days you will have ripe grapes.'

Thereupon he returned home and told his mother how he had met the little girl, and what she had told him; not, however, as having any belief in what she had said. The mother, however, when she had heard his words, said, 'Go, my son, and try; anyhow you are a lost man. You can but try.'

He went then to the king and demanded land for the vineyard, and begged that it should be dug in straight rows. The king ordered everything to be done as the young man demanded, who forthwith took a sack on his shoulder, and a sprig of basilicum, and went full of fear and sorrow to lie down in the place. When he awoke next morning the vines were already planted; the second morning the leaves were on the vines; and, in short, on the seventh day there were ripe grapes, and that, too, in a season when grapes were to be found nowhere else.

He gathered some grapes, and made sweet wine; and took also a cluster of grapes in a handkerchief, and went to the king.

The king and the whole court were exceedingly surprised, but the young man's uncle said, 'Now we will order him to do something which it is quite impossible that he should do.' He then advised the king to call the young man, and order him to make a palace of elephants' tusks.

The young man heard the king's order, and went home weeping. He told his mother the order which the king had given him, and said, 'Mother, this is a task which neither I nor any one else can fulfil.' Then the mother advised him to take a walk beyond the village. 'Perhaps,' said she, 'you will again meet the little girl.' Accordingly he went; and when he reached the place where he had before seen the maiden, she again appeared to him, and said, 'You are sad and troubled as before, my brother.' Then he told her what a task the king had set him to perform. She, however, no sooner heard this than she said, 'This will also be easy; but first go to the king, and demand from him a ship with three hundred barrels of wine, and three hundred barrels of brandy, and twenty carpenters. Then, when you arrive at a place which you will find between the mountains, dam up the water there, and pour into it the wine and the brandy. The elephants will soon come there to drink water, and will get drunk and fall down. Then your twenty carpenters must cut off their tusks, and carry them to the spot where the king desires to have the palace built. Then lie down there to sleep, and in seven days the palace will be ready.'

The young man returned home and told his mother what the young maiden had said to him. The mother advised him to follow the girl's counsel. 'Go, my son,' she said, 'perhaps God will again help you.' So the young man went to the king, and demanded the barrels of wine and brandy, and the twenty carpenters. The king furnished him with all he desired; and he went immediately where the girl had told him, and did as she had ordered. And, even as she had foretold, the elephants came to drink, and got tipsy, and fell down; and the carpenters sawed their tusks, and carried them to the spot where the palace was to be built. Then, at evening, the young man took his sack and a branch of basilicum, and went and lay down to sleep in the place.

And on the seventh day the palace was ready. When the king saw it, he marvelled, and said to his first minister, the uncle of the young man, 'Now what shall we do with him? Indeed he is not a man; God knows only what he is.'

To this, the minister answered, 'Yet one thing you ought to order him to do, and if he fulfils that, also, indeed he must be something more than man.' So, in accordance with the advice of his minister, the king called the young man again, and said, 'Now, go and bring me the king's daughter from such and such a kingdom, and out of such a city. If you should fail to bring her, you will lose your head.'

The young man went home and told his mother the new task which the king had set him to do, and the mother said, 'Go, my son, and look for that young maiden. Perhaps God will grant that she may save you a third time!'

So, as before, he went outside the village, and met the young maiden, and told her what he had now to do.

The girl listened to him, and then said, 'Go and demand from the king a ship; in the ship must be made twenty shops, and in each shop must be a different kind of ware, each one better than the other. Then demand that the twenty handsomest young men should be chosen, and finely dressed, and put one in each shop as salesman. Then sail yourself with the ship, and you will first meet a man who carries a large eagle. You must ask him if he will sell it you, and he will answer "Yes." Then give him anything he demands in return for the eagle. After that you will meet a man carrying in his fishing-net a carp with golden scales; you must buy the carp, whatever it may cost you. Thirdly, you will meet a man carrying a live dove, and this dove you must also buy, whatever the price may be. Then, take a feather from the eagle's tail, a scale from the carp, and a little feather from the left wing of the dove, and let the eagle, carp, and dove go away free. When you arrive in the kingdom, and at the city where the princess resides, you must open all the twenty shops, and order each young man to stand before his shop-door. Then the citizens will come and admire the wares; and the maidens, who come to fetch water, will go back into the city and say, "Such a ship and such wares were never before seen since this was a city!" This news will reach the ears of the king's daughter, and she will beg permission from her father to go and see the ship herself. When she comes, with her friends, on board, you must lead her from one shop to the other, and bring out and show her the finest wares which you have. Thus you must contrive to engage her attention and to keep her on board till it gets dusk, and then let the ship sail. In that moment it will be so dark that nothing can be seen. The girl will have a bird on her shoulder, and, when she sees the ship is sailing away, she will let the bird fly to take tiding to the palace of what has happened to her. Then you must burn the eagle's plume, and the old eagle will instantly come to you. You must order him to catch the bird, and he will quickly do so. Then the girl will throw a small stone into the water, and the ship will at once stand still; but you will immediately burn the carp's scale, and the carp will come to you. You must order him to find and swallow that little water of life, and when he does so the ship will sail on. After sailing some time you will arrive between two mountains; there the ship will turn to stone and you will be greatly terrified. The girl will urge you to fetch some water of life, and you must then burn the dove's feather, and the bird will immediately appear. You will give him a little bottle that he may bring you some water of life, and when he does so the ship will sail on again, and you will come happily home with the king's daughter.'

The young man listened to the advice of the maiden, and then returned home and told all to his mother. After that he went to the king and demanded all the things that the maiden had counselled him to procure. The king could not refuse, so all that he asked was given him, and he sailed away.

All things happened exactly as the young maiden had foretold, and the young man came back with the king's daughter happily to his own country.

The king and his first minister, the uncle of the young man, saw, from the windows of the palace, the ship whilst yet it was far from the city; and the minister said to the king, 'Now there is nothing left to do but to kill him as he comes out of the ship!' When the ship reached the port, the king's daughter first came ashore with her companions; then the handsome young shopmen, and, lastly, the young man alone. But the king had had the headsman placed there, and when the young man stepped on the shore the executioner cut his head off. The king intended to marry the king's daughter; accordingly, as soon as she came on land he ran to her, and began to caress her, but she turned away her head from him, and said, 'Where is he who has been working for me?' And when she saw that his head was cut off she rushed to the body, took out some water of life and poured over it, so he arose alive and well as ever. When the king and his minister saw this wonder, the minister said to the king, ' This man will know now more than ever he did, since he has been dead and is come back to life!' Then the king began to wonder if it were true that a man who has been dead knows more when he returns to life, and, in order to satisfy his curiosity, he ordered the headsman to cut off his head, and directed that the girl with the water of life should bring him again to life. But, after the king's head was cut off, the girl refused to restore him to life. Instead of doing so, she wrote a letter to her father, told him all that had happened, and told him her wish to marry the young man. So the king, her father, sent forth a proclamation that the people should take the young man for their king, and threatened to declare war against them if they refused to do so. The people recognised immediately the merits of the young man, and owned that he deserved to be their king, and to marry the king's daughter. Accordingly they made him king, and he married the king's daughter. Then the handsome young men, who had sailed with him in the ship as shopmen, married the companions of the king's daughter who was now queen, and thus all of them became great dignitaries in the kingdom.

WHO ASKS LITTLE, GETS MUCH.

ONCE on a time there lived three brothers, who had no property except one pear-tree. This they watched carefully, each of them in turn guarding it, whilst the other two worked for wages away from home. One day God sent an angel to see how these brothers were living; and ordered the angel, if they lived very poorly, to give them better food. When the angel came down to the earth, he changed himself into the form of a beggar; and when he saw one of the brothers watching the pear-tree, asked him to give him a pear. Then the brother plucked some pears, and gave them to the beggar, and said, 'Here, take these from my share of the pears; I cannot give you any of those which belong to my brothers.' So the angel thanked the man and went away.

Next morning the second brother remained to guard the pear-tree; and the angel came again, and begged him to give him a pear. The man took some of the pears and gave them to the angel, saying, 'Take these from my pears; but from the pears of my brothers I dare not give you any.'

The third day the third brother stayed at home to watch the pear tree, and the angel came as before, and asked only for one pear. And this brother said also, 'Here are some of my pears; from the pears of my brothers I cannot give you any.'

The day after, the angel changed himself into a monk, and came very early, so that he found all three brothers at home, and said to them, 'Come with me; I will give you better nourishment than you have at present.'

The three brothers followed him without saying a word. At last they came to a large torrent, where the water flowed in great streams, and made a loud noise. Then the angel asked the eldest brother, 'What would you like?' And the man answered, 'I should like all this water to be changed into wine, and to belong to me.'

Then the angel made the sign of the cross in the air with his stick, and, in a moment, wine was flowing instead of water. On the banks of the river heaps of barrels were being made, and men were working very diligently —in short, there was quite a village. The angel then left the eldest brother there, saying, 'Here is all you wished! now keep yourself!' and he continued his journey with the other two brothers. Then they came to a field covered over with a multitude of doves, and the angel asked the second brother, 'What would you like?' 'I should like all these doves to be sheep, and to belong to me!' replied the man. The angel again made the sign of the cross in the air with his stick, and, instantly, sheep were there instead of doves. There were dairies also, and women milking the sheep; some were pouring out the milk, and others collecting the cream; some were making cheese, others churning butter. There was also a slaughter-house, with men cutting the meat into joints, whilst others were weighing it, and others receiving money as they sold the meat.

Then the angel said to the second brother, 'Here, is what you wished for; now live.' The angel now took with him the youngest brother, walked with him across the field, and then asked, 'And what would *you* like?' The man answered, 'I wish for nothing, except that God may give me a wife of pure Christian blood!' Then the angel said, 'Oh, that is difficult to find! In the whole world there are but three such, and two of them are already married. The third is a maid still, but she is asked in marriage by two wooers.'

So the angel and the young man set out, and, having journeyed a long way, at length came to the city where the king dwelt whose daughter was of pure Christian blood.

As soon as they arrived, they went to the palace to ask for the girl. When they entered the palace, they found two kings already there, and their wedding gifts laid out upon a table. Then they also placed there the presents they had brought. When the king saw them, he said to all those who were standing before him, 'What shall we do now? Those are the presents of kings, but these look, in comparison, like the gifts of a beggar!' Then the angel said, 'I will tell you what to do. Let the matter be decided in this way—the maid shall take three vines, and plant them in the garden, dedicating each of them to one of the three wooers. The man on whose vine grapes are found next day is the one the girl ought to marry.' So all agreed to this, and the maid planted three vines in the garden, dedicating each of them to one of her three wooers.

The next morning, when they looked, grapes were found on the vine dedicated to the poor man. So the king could not help himself, and was obliged to give his daughter to the youngest brother, and let them at once be married in the church. After the wedding, the angel took them to a forest, and left them there, where they lived for a whole year.

At the end of a year, God again sent the angel, saying, 'Go down and see how those poor men are living. If their food be scanty, give them better nourishment.'

The angel came down to earth as before, in the likeness of a beggar, and went first to the brother who had the torrent overflowing with wine. The beggar asked for a cup of wine, but the man refused, saying, 'If I were to give every one who asks a cup of wine, I should have none for myself!' When the angel heard this, he made the sign of the cross with his stick, and the torrent began to flow with water as at first. Then the angel said to the eldest brother, 'That was not for thee! go back under the pear-tree and guard it!'

After that the angel went to the second brother who

had the field quite covered with sheep, and begged him to give him a morsel of cheese; but he refused, saying, 'If I were to give every one a little bit of cheese, I should have none left!' When the angel heard this, he made the sign of the cross in the air, and the sheep turned in an instant into doves, and flew away.

Then the angel said to the second brother, 'That was not for thee! go back under the pear-tree and guard it!'

At last the angel went to see how the youngest brother was living, and found him with his wife in the forest, dwelling in a little hut, and living poorly. He begged to be allowed to sleep there that night, and they received him with great willingness, only excusing themselves that they could not serve him as they would. 'We are only poor people,' they said. The angel answered, 'Do not speak about that! I shall be quite content with what you have for yourselves.' Then these poor people asked themselves what they must do. They had no corn to make real bread; for they usually ground the bark of certain trees, and made bread from it. Such bread, therefore, the wife made now for their guest, and put it to the fire to bake. Whilst it baked, they talked with him. In a little while, when they looked to see whether the cake was baked, they found that there was a loaf of real bread quite ready for the table, and very large. When they saw that, they lifted up their hands and thanked God, saying, 'Thank thee, O God! that we are now able to give food to our guest.'

So they placed the bread before the angel, and also filled a vessel with water, and when they came to drink they found it was wine. Then the angel made a sign of the cross with his staff over the hut, and on that spot rose a royal palace, filled with abundance of everything. And the angel blessed the youngest brother and his wife, and left them, and they lived there long and very happily.

JUSTICE OR INJUSTICE? WHICH IS BEST.

A KING had two sons; of these, one was cunning and unjust, the other, just and gentle. After the death of the father the elder son said to the younger, 'Depart; I will not live with you any longer. Here are three hundred zechins and a horse: this is your portion of our father's property. Take it, for I owe you nothing more than this.' The younger son took the money and the horse which were offered him, and said, 'Thank God! See only how much of the kingdom has fallen to me!'

Some time afterwards the two brothers, both of whom were riding, met by chance in a road. The younger brother greeted the elder one, saying, 'God help thee, brother!' and the elder answered, 'Why do you speak always about God? Nowadays, injustice is better than justice.' The younger brother, however, said to him, 'I will wager with you that injustice is not, as you say, better than justice.' So they betted one hundred golden zechins, and it was arranged that they should leave the decision to the first man they met in the road. Riding together a little farther they met with Satan, who had disguised himself as a monk, and they asked him to decide which was better, justice or injustice? Satan answered, 'Injustice!' And the good brother paid the bad one the hundred golden zechins which he had wagered.

Then they betted for another hundred zechins, and again a third time for a third hundred, and each time Satan—who managed to disguise himself in different ways and meet them—decided that injustice was better than justice.

Thus the younger brother lost all his money, and his horse into the bargain. Then he said, 'Thank God! I have no more money, but I have eyes, and I wager my eyes that justice is better than injustice.'

Thereupon the unjust brother, without waiting for any one's decision, drew his knife and cut both his brother's eyes out, saying, 'Now you have no eyes, let justice help you.' But the younger brother in his trouble only thanked God and said, 'I have lost my eyes for the sake of God's justice, but I pray you, my brother, give me a little water in some vessel to wash my wounds and wet my mouth, and bring me away from this place to the pine-tree just about the spring, before you leave me.' The unjust brother did so, gave him water, and left him alone under the pine-tree near the spring of water.

There the unfortunate remained, sitting on the ground. Late, however, in the night, some fairies came to the spring to bathe, and one of them said to the others, 'Do you know, my sisters, that the king' daughter has got the leprosy? The king has summoned all the physicians, but no one can possibly help her. But if the king only knew, he would take a little of this water in which we are bathing, and wash his daughter therewith! and then in a day and a night she would recover completely from her leprosy. Just as any one deaf, or dumb, or blind, could be cured by this same water.'

Then, as the cocks began to crow, the fairies hurried away. As soon as they were gone, the unfortunate man felt his way slowly with his outstretched hands till he came to the spring of water. There he bathed his eyes, and in an instant recovered his sight. After that he filled the vessel with water, and hurried away to the king, whose daughter was leprous, and said to the servants, 'I am come to cure the king's daughter, if he will only let me try. I guarantee that she will become healthy in a day and night.'

When the king heard that, he ordered him to be led into the room where the girl was, and made her immediately bathe in the water. After a day and a night the the girl came out pure and healthy.

Then the king was greatly pleased, and gave the young prince the half of his kingdom, and also his daughter for a wife, so that he became the king's son-in-law, and the first man after him in the kingdom.

The tidings of this great event spread all over the world, and so came to the ears of the unjust brother. He guessed directly that his blind brother must have met with good fortune under the pine-tree, so he went himself to try to find it also. He carried with him a vessel full of water, and then carved out his own eyes with his knife. When it was dark the fairies came again, and, as they bathed, spoke about the recovery of the king's daughter. 'It cannot be otherwise,' they said, 'someone must have been listening to our last conversation here. Perhaps someone is listening now. Let us see.'

So they searched all around, and when they came to the pine-tree they found there the unjust brother who had come to seek after good fortune, and who declared always that injustice was better than justice. They immediately caught him, and tore him into four parts.

And so, at the last, his wickedness did not help him, and he found to his cost that justice is better than injustice.

SATAN'S JUGGLINGS AND GOD'S MIGHT.

ONE morning the son of the king went out to hunt. Whilst walking through the snow he cut himself a little, and the drops of blood fell on the snow. When he saw how pretty the red blood looked on the white snow, he thought, 'Oh, if I could only marry a girl as white as snow and as rosy red as this blood!' Whilst he was thus thinking, he met an old woman and asked her if there were such maidens anywhere to be found. The old woman told him that on the mountain he saw before him he would find a house without doors, and the only entrance and outlet of this house was a single window. And she added, 'In that house, my son, there is living a girl such as you desire; but of the young men who have gone to ask her to be their wife none have returned.'

'That may all be as you say,' answered the prince, 'I will go, nevertheless! Only tell me the way that I must take to get to the house.' When the old woman heard this resolve, she was sorry for the young man, and, taking a piece of bread from her pouch, she gave it to him, saying, 'Take this bread and keep it safe as the apple of your eye!' The prince took the bread, and continued his journey. Very soon afterwards he met another old woman, and she asked him where he was going. He told her he was going to demand the girl who lived in the doorless house on the mountain. Then the old woman tried to dissuade him, telling him just the same things as the former one had done. He said, however, 'That may be quite true, nevertheless I will go, even if I never return.' Then the old woman gave to the prince a little nut, saying, 'Keep this nut always by you; it may help you some time or other!'

The prince took the nut and went on his way, till he came to where an old woman was sitting by the roadside. She asked him, 'Where are you going?' Then he told her he was going to demand the girl who lived in the house on the mountain before him. Upon this the old woman wept, and prayed him to give up all thoughts of the girl, and she gave him the very same warnings as the other old women had done. All this however was of no use, the prince was resolved to go on, so the old woman gave him a walnut, saying, 'Take this walnut, and keep it carefully until you want it.'

He wondered at these presents, and asked her to tell him why the first old woman had given him a piece of bread, the second a nut, and she herself now a walnut. The old woman answered, 'The bread is to throw to the beasts before the house, that they may not eat you; and, when you find yourself in the greatest danger, ask counsel, first from the nut, and then from the walnut.'

Then the king's son continued his wandering, till he came at last to a thick forest, in the midst of which he saw the house with only a single window. When he came near it he was attacked by a multitude of beasts of all kinds, and, following the advice of the old woman, he threw the bit of bread towards them. Then the beasts came and smelt at the bread one after the other, and, upon doing so, each drew his tail between his legs and lay down quietly.

The house had no door, and but one window, which was very high above the ground, so high that do what he could he was not able to reach it. Suddenly he saw a woman letting down her golden hair; so he rushed and caught hold of it, and she drew him up thereby into the house. Then he saw that the woman was she for whose sake he had come to this place. The prince and the girl were equally pleased to see each other, and she said, 'Thank God that my mother happened to be from home! She is gone into the forest to gather the plants by the aid of which she transforms into beasts all the young men who venture here to ask me to be their wife. Those are the beasts who would have killed you, if God had not helped you. But let us fly away from this place. So they fled away through the forest as quickly as they could. As they happened to look back, however, they saw that the girl's mother was pursuing them, and they became frightened. The old woman was already very near them before the prince remembered his nut. He took it out quickly and asked, 'For God's sake! tell me what we must do now?' The nut replied,

'Open me!' The prince opened it, and from the little nut flowed out a large river, which stopped the way, so that for a time the girl's mother could not pass. However, she touched the waters with her staff, and they immediately divided and left her a dry path, so that she could run on quickly after the prince and the girl.

When the prince saw she would soon come up with them, he took out the walnut and asked, 'Tell me, what we must do now?' And the walnut replied, 'Break me!' The king's son broke the walnut, and a great fire flamed out from it—so great a fire that the whole forest barely escaped being consumed by it. But the girl's mother spat on the fire, and it extinguished itself in a moment. Then the king's son saw that these were nothing but the jugglings of the devil, so he turned eastward, made the sign of the cross, and called on the mighty God to help him. Then it suddenly thundered and lightened, and from heaven flashed a thunderbolt which struck the mother of the girl, and she fell dead upon the ground.

Thus at length the king's son arrived safely at home, and when the girl had been made a Christian, he married her.

THE WISE GIRL.

ONCE upon a time a poor man lived in a small and mean cottage. He possessed nothing in the world except a daughter who was very wise indeed. She taught her father how to beg, and how to speak wisely. One day the poor man went to the king to beg, and the king asked him whence he came, and who had taught him to speak so well.

He told the king where he lived, and that he had a daughter who told him what to say.

'And who taught your daughter all this wisdom?' demanded the king. The poor man answered, 'God and our poverty have made her wise.'

Then the king gave him thirty eggs and said, 'Take these eggs to your daughter, and tell her that if she bring forth chickens from the eggs, I will make her rich presents; but if she fails, then I will have you tortured.'

The poor man went back to his cottage weeping, and told all this to his daughter. The girl saw at once that the eggs which the king had sent had been boiled, but she told her father to go to sleep quietly, and she would take care for everything. The father did as she said, and, whilst he slept, she took a pot, filled it with water and beans, and boiled them.

Next morning she told her father to take a plough and oxen, and go to plough in a wood near to which the king would pass. 'When you see the king coming,' said she, 'take a handful of beans, and begin to sow, shouting, "Go on, my oxen, and God grant that the boiled beans may bear fruit!" When the kings asks you, "How can you expect boiled beans to grow?" answer him, "Just as much as from boiled eggs to hatch chickens!"'

The poor man listened to his daughter, and went to plough. When the king came near, he began to shout, 'Ho ho, my oxen! go on! and God grant that these boiled beans may bring me a good crop!'

The king, hearing these words, stopped his carriage, and said to the poor man, 'Poor fellow, how can boiled beans bear a crop?'

'Just as well as boiled eggs can bring forth chickens,' answered the man.

The king saw that his daughter had taught him what to say, and he ordered his servants to bring the man before him. Then the king gave him a bunch of flax, saying, 'Take this, and make from it all the sails a ship needs. If you do not, you shall lose your life.'

The poor man took the bunch of flax with great fear, and returned weeping to the cottage to tell his daughter, who bade him go to sleep quietly. Next morning she gave him a small piece of wood, and told him to take it to the king and demand that, from this piece of wood, all the tools needful for spinning and weaving should be made. 'Then,' continued she, 'I will make all that he has ordered me.'

The king was surprised, and considered a moment what to do. At last he said, 'Take this little glass to your daughter, and tell her she must empty the sea with it, so that dry land shall be where the water now is.'

The poor man took the little cup to his daughter, and, weeping, told her all the king required. The girl bade him be quiet till morning, and then she would do all that was needed. Next morning she called her father, gave him a pound of tow, and said, 'Take this to the king, and tell him that with this tow he must first stop all the sources of the rivers and lakes, and then I will dry up the sea.'

So the poor man went to the king and told him what has daughter had said.

The king, seeing that the girl was wiser than himself, ordered that she should be brought before him. When she bent before the king, he said, 'Guess, maiden! what can be heard at the greatest distance?'

The girl answered, 'Your majesty, the thunder and the lie can be heard at the greatest distance.'

Then the king grasped his beard, and, turning to his courtiers, put to them the question, 'Guess what my beard is worth? Some of them said so much, others again so much; but the girl observed to the king that none of the courtiers had guessed right, and said, 'The king s beard is worth as much as three summer rains.' The king, greatly astonished, said, 'It is so; the girl has guessed rightly!' Then he asked her if she were willing to be his wife; and added that, if she were willing, he would marry her.

The girl bent low and said, 'Let it be as your majesty commands! But I pray you write with your hand on a scrap of paper this promise, that if you should ever be displeased with me, and should send me away from you, I shall be allowed to take with me from the palace any one thing which I like best.'

The king consented, and gave the promise.

After they had lived happily together for some time, one day the king was angry, and said to his wife, 'I will not have you any longer for my wife, and I bid you leave the palace!'

The queen answered, 'I will obey your majesty, but permit me to pass one night more in the palace. To-morrow I will go.'

This, the king could not well refuse.

That evening, at supper, the queen mixed something with the wine, and offered it to the king to drink, saying, 'Be of good cheer, O king! To-morrow we shall separate and, believe me, I shall be happier than I was when I first met you.'

The king drank, and soon after fell asleep. Then the queen ordered her carriage, and carried the king away with her to the cottage.

Next morning, when the king awoke in the cottage and saw where he was, he exclaimed, 'Who brought me here?'

The queen answered, 'I brought you.'

Then the king asked, 'How have you dared to do so? Did I not tell you I will not have you any longer for my wife?'

But the queen took out the king's written promise, and said, 'Yes, indeed, you told me so; but see, you have written and promised that I "shall be allowed to take with me from the palace that which I like best, whenever I must leave the court."'

The king, seeing the paper, kissed his wife, and returned with her to the palace.

GOOD DEEDS ARE NEVER LOST.

IN days gone by there lived a married couple who had one only son. When he grew up they made him learn something which would be of use to him in after-life. He was a kind, quiet boy, and feared God greatly. After his schooling was finished his father gave him a ship, freighted with various sorts of merchandise, so that he might go and trade about the world, and grow rich, and become a help to his parents in their old age. The son put to sea, and one day the ship he was in met with a Turkish vessel in which he heard great weeping and wailing. So he demanded of the Turkish sailors, 'Pray, tell me why there is so much wailing on board your ship?' and they answered, 'We are carrying slaves which we have captured in different countries, and those who are chained are weeping.'

Then he said, 'Please, brothers, ask your captain if he would give me the slaves for ready cash?'

The captain gladly agreed to the proposal, and after much bargaining the young man gave to the captain his vessel full of merchandise, and received in exchange the ship full of slaves.

Then he called the slaves before him, and demanded

of each whence he came, and told them all they were free to return to their own countries. At last he came to an old woman who held close to her side a very beautiful girl, and he asked them from what country they came. The old woman told him, weeping, that they came from a very distant land, saying, 'This young girl is the only daughter of the king, and I am her nurse, and have taken care of her from her childhood. One day, unhappily, she went to walk in a garden far away from the palace, and these wicked Turks saw her and caught her. Luckily I happened to be near, and, hearing her scream, ran to her help, and so the Turks caught me too, and brought us both on board of this ship.' Then the old woman and the beautiful girl, being so far from their own country, and having no means of getting there, begged him that he would take them with him. So he married the girl, took her with him, and returned home.

When he arrived his father asked him about his ship and merchandise, and he told him what had happened, how he had given his vessel with its cargo, and had bought the slaves and set them free. 'This girl,' continued he, 'is a king's daughter, and the old woman her nurse; as they could not get back to their country, they prayed to remain with me, so I married the girl.'

Thereupon the father was very angry, and said, 'My foolish son! what have you done? Why have you made away with my property without cause and of your own will?' and he drove him out of the house.

Then the son lived with his wife and her old nurse

a long time in the same village, trying always, through the good offices of his mother and other friends, to obtain his father's forgiveness, and, begging him to let him have a second ship full of merchandise, promised to be wiser in future. After some time the father took pity on him, and received him again into his house, with his wife and her old nurse. Shortly after he fitted him out another ship, larger than the first one, and filled with more valuable merchandise. In this he sailed, leaving his wife and her nurse in the house of his parents. He came one day to a city where he found the soldiers very busy carrying some unlucky villagers away to prison. So he asked them, 'Why are you doing this my brethren? Why are you driving these poor people to prison?' and the soldiers answered:

'They have not paid the king's taxes, that is why we take them to prison.'

Then he went to the magistrate and asked, 'Please tell me how much these poor prisoners owe?'

When the magistrate told him he sold his goods and ship, and paid the debts of all the prisoners, and returned home without anything. Falling at the feet of his father, he told him what he had done, and begged him to forgive him. But the father was exceedingly angry, more so than before, and drove him away from his presence. What could the unhappy son do in this great strait? How could he go begging, he whose parents were so rich? After some time his friends again prevailed upon the father to receive him back, because, as they urged, so much suffering had made him wiser. At last the father yielded, took him again into his house, and prepared a ship for him finer and richer than the two former ones. Then the son had the portrait of his wife painted on the helm, and that of the old nurse on the stern, and, after taking leave of his father and mother, and wife, he sailed away the third time.

After sailing for some days he came near a large city, in which there lived a king, and, dropping anchor, he fired a salute to the city. All the citizens wondered, as did also their king, and no one could say who the captain of the strange ship might be. In the afternoon the king sent one of his ministers to ask who he was, and why he came; and the minister brought a message that the king himself would come at nine o'clock the next morning to see the ship. When the minister came he saw on the helm the portrait of the king's daughter, and on the stern that of her old nurse, and in his surprise and joy dared not believe his own eyes. For the princess had been promised to him in marriage while she was yet a child, and long before she was captured by the Turks.

But the minister did not tell any one what he had seen.

Next morning, at nine o'clock, the king came with his ministers on board the ship, and asked the captain who he was, and whence he came?

Whilst walking about the vessel he saw there the portrait of the girl on the helm and that of the old woman on the stern, and recognised the features of his own daughter and her old nurse who had been captured by the Turks. But his joy was so great, he dared not believe his eyes, so he invited the captain to come that afternoon to his palace to relate his adventures, hoping thus to find out if his hopes were well founded.

In the afternoon, in obedience to the king's wish, he went to the palace, and the king at once began to inquire why the figure of the girl was painted on the helm and that of the old woman on the stern. The captain guessed at once that this king must be his wife's father, so he told him everything that had happened—how he had met the Turkish ship filled with slaves, and had ransomed them and set them free. 'This girl, alone,' he continued, 'with her old nurse, had nowhere to go, as her country was so far off, so they asked to remain with me, and I married the girl.'

When the king heard this he exclaimed, 'That girl is my only child, and the accursed Turks took her and her old nurse. You, since you are her husband, will be the heir to my crown. But go—go at once to your home and bring me your wife that I may see her—my only daughter, before I die. Bring your father, your mother, bring all your family. Let your property be all sold in that country, and come all of you here. Your father shall be my brother, and your mother my sister, as you are my son and the heir to my crown. We will all live together here in one palace.' Then he called the queen, and all his ministers, and told them all about his daughter. And there was great rejoicing and festivity in the whole court.

After this the king gave his son-in-law his own large ship to bring back the princess and the whole family. So the captain left his own ship there, but he asked the king to send one of his ministers with him, 'Lest they should not believe me,' he said; and the king gave him as a companion for his voyage the same minister to whom he had formerly promised the princess in marriage. They arrived safely in port, and the captain's father was surprised to see his son return so soon, and with such a splendid vessel.

Then he told all that had happened and his mother and wife, and especially the old nurse, rejoiced greatly when they heard the good news. As the king's minister was there to witness the truth of this strange news, no one could doubt it. So the father and mother consented to sell all their property and go to live in the king's palace.

But the minister resolved to kill this new heir to the king and husband of the princess who had been promised to him for wife; so, when they had sailed a long distance, he called him on deck to confer with him. The captain had a quiet conscience, and did not suspect any evil, so he came up at once, and the minister caught him quickly and threw him overboard

The ship was sailing fast, and it was rather dark, so the captain could not overtake her, but was left behind in the deep waters. The minister, however, went quietly to sleep.

Fortunately the waves carried the king's young heir to a rock near the shore: it was, however, a desert country, and no one was near to help him. Those he had left on board the ship, seeing next morning that he had disappeared, began to weep and wail, thinking he had fallen overboard in the night and been drowned. His wife especially lamented him, because they had loved each other very much. When the ship arrived at the king's city, and reported to him the great disaster that had befallen them, the king was troubled, and the whole court mourned greatly. The king kept the parents and family of the young man by him as he had engaged to do, but they could not console themselves for their great loss.

Meanwhile, the king's unhappy son-in-law sat on the rock, and lived on the moss which grew there, and was scorched by the hot sun, from which he had no shelter; his garments were soiled and torn, and no one would have recognised him. Still not a living soul was to be seen anywhere to help him. At last, after fifteen days and fifteen nights, he noticed an old man on the shore, leaning on a staff, and engaged in fishing. Then the king's heir shouted to the old man, and begged him to help him off the rock. The old fisherman consented—

'If you will pay me for it,' said he.

'How can I pay you when, as you see, I have nothing, and even my clothes are only rags?' answered the young man sadly.

'Oh, that matters nothing,' exclaimed the old man; 'I have here pen and paper, so, if you know how to use them, write a promise to give me half of everything you may ever possess, and then sign the paper.'

To that the young man gladly consented; so the old man walked through the water to him, and he signed the paper, and then the old man took him over to the shore. After that he journeyed from village to village, barefoot, hungry, and sorrowful, and begged some garments to cover him.

After thirty days' wandering, his good luck led him to the city of the king, and he went and sat at the door of the palace, wearing on his finger his wedding-ring, on which was his own name and the name of his wife. At eventide, the king's servants took him into the courtyard, and gave him to eat what remained of their supper. Next morning he took his stand by the garden-door, but the gardener came and drove him away, saying that the king and his family were soon coming that way. So he moved away a little, and sat down near a corner of the garden and shortly afterward he saw the king walking with his mother, his father leading the queen, and his wife walking with the minister, his great enemy. He did not yet desire to show himself to them, but as they passed near him and gave him alms, his wife saw the wedding-ring on a finger of the hand which he held out to take the money. Still she could not think the beggar could be her husband, so she said—

'Let me see the ring you have on your finger.'

The minister, who was walking by her, was a little frightened, and said—

'Go on, how can you speak to that ragged beggar?'

But she would not hear him. She took the ring, and read thereon her own and her husband's names. Her heart was greatly troubled by the sight of the ring, but she controlled her feelings and said nothing. As soon as they returned to the palace, she told the king, her father, that she had recognised her husband's ring on the hand of the beggar who sat by the side of the garden. 'So please send for him,' said she, 'that we may find out how the ring came into his hands.'

Then the king sent his servants to find the beggar, and they brought him to the palace. And the king asked him whence he came, and how he got that ring. Then he could no longer restrain himself, but told them how he had been thrown overboard by the treacherous minister, and spent fifteen days and nights on the naked rock, and how he had been saved.

'You see now how God and my right-dealing have brought me back to my parents and my wife.'

When they heard that, they could hardly speak, so rejoiced were they. Then the king summoned the father and mother, and related what had happened to their son.

The servants quickly brought him fine new garments, and bathed and clothed him. Then for many days there was great rejoicings, not only in the palace, but also in all the city, and he was crowned as king. The minister was seized by the king's order, and given up to the king's son-in-law, that he might punish him after his own will. But the young king would not permit him to be put to death, but forgave him, on condition that he left the kingdom instantly.

A few days after, the old man who had saved the

young king came, bringing with him his written promise. The young king took the paper, and reading it, said—

'My old man, sit down. To-day I am king, but if I were a beggar I would fulfil my word, and acknowledge my signature. Therefore we will divide all that I have.'

So he took out the book and began to divide the cities.

'This is for me—that is for you.' So saying, he wrote all on a chart, till all were divided between them, from the greatest city to the poorest barrack.

The old man accepted his half, but immediately made a present of it again to the young king, saying—

'Take it! I am not an old man, but an angel from God! I was sent by God to save thee, for the sake of thy good deeds. Now reign and be happy, and may thy prosperity last long.'

The angel disappeared; and the king reigned there in great happiness.

LYING FOR A WAGER.

ONE day a father sent his son to the mill with corn to grind; but before he went he recommended him not to grind it in the mill in which he should happen to meet with a man named 'Beardless.'† The boy came to a mill, but there he found Beardless.

'God bless you, Beardless,' said he.

'God bless you too, my son,' replied the man.

'Can I grind my corn here?' asked the boy.

'Why not?' responded Beardless; 'my corn will be soon ready, and you can grind yours as long as you like.'

But the boy recollected his father's advice, and left the mill and went to another. But Beardless took some corn, and hurried by a shorter way, to the mill towards which the boy had gone, and reached there before him, and put some of his corn into the mill to be ground. When the boy arrived, he was greatly surprised to find Beardless there, and so he went away from this and approached a third mill. But Beardless hurried by a short cut, and reached this mill also before the boy, and gave some of his corn to be ground. He did the same at a fourth mill; so the boy got tired, and,

† The 'Beardless,' in Serbian national tales, is the personification of craft and sharpness.

thinking that he should find Beardless in every mill, put down his sack, and resolved to grind in this mill, although Beardless was there.

When the boy's corn came to be ground, Beardless said to him, 'Hearken, my son. Let us make a cake of your flour.'

The boy was thinking all the time of his father's words, but he could not help himself. So he said, 'Very good, we will make one.'

Beardless got up and began to mix the flour with water, which the boy brought him, and he kept mixing till all the corn was ground, and all the flour made into a very large loaf. Then they made a fire, put the bread to bake, and, when it was baked, took it and placed it against a wall.

Then Beardless said, 'My son, listen to me. If we were to divide the loaf between us, it would not be enough for either of us, so let us tell each other some lies, and whoever tells the greatest lie shall have the whole loaf for himself.'

The boy thought, 'I cannot now draw back, so I may as well do my best and go on.' So he said aloud to Beardless, 'Very well, but you must begin.'

Then Beardless told many different lies, and when he got quite tired of lying, the boy said to him, 'Eh! my dear Beardless, if that is all you know, it is not much. Only listen, and have patience a little, whilst I tell you a real truth. In my *young* days, when I was an *old* man, we had very many beehives, and it was my business every morning to count them. Now I always counted the bees easily enough, but I never could count the beehives. One morning, whilst counting the bees, I saw that the best bee was missing, so I put a saddle on the cock and mounted, and started in search of my bee. I traced it to the sea-shore, and saw that it had gone over the sea, so I followed it. When I got over, I saw that a man had caught my bee, and was ploughing a field with it in which he was about to sow millet. I called to him, "That is my bee! How did you get her?" And the man said, "Well, brother, if it is yours, take it." And he gave me back my bee, and also a sack full of millet. Then I put the sack on my back, and moved the saddle from the cock to the bee. Then I mounted it, and led the cock behind me, that he might rest a little. Whilst I was crossing the sea, somehow one of the strings of the sack broke, and all the millet fell into the water.

'When I had got over it was already night, so I dismounted and let the bee loose to graze. The cock I fastened near me, and gave him some hay; after that I lay down to sleep. When I awoke in the morning, I found the wolves had killed my bee and eaten it up; and the honey was lying all about the valley ankle-deep; and on the hills it lay knee-deep. Then I began to think in what I could gather up all the honey. I remembered I had a little axe by me, so I went into the forest to try to kill some beast, in order to make a sack from its skin. In the forest I saw two deer dancing on one leg; so I broke the leg with my little axe and caught them both. From the two deer I drew three skins and made three bags, wherein I gathered up all the honey. I put the sacks full of honey on the cock's back, and hastened home. When I reached home I found that my father had just been born, and they sent me to heaven to bring some holy water. Whilst I was thinking how I should go up to heaven, I remembered the millet which had fallen into the sea. When I reached the sea I found the millet had grown up quite to heaven, so I climbed it and reached the sky. And on getting into heaven I saw the millet was quite ripe, and that one whom I met there had reaped it, and had already made a loaf from it, and had broken some pieces into warm milk, which he was eating. I greeted him, saying, "God help you!" and he answered, "God help thee also!" and then he gave me holy water and I returned. But I found that meanwhile there had been a great rain, so that the sea had risen and carried away my millet. Then I grew very anxious as to how I should get down again to earth. At last I remembered that I have long hair, so long that when I stand upright it reaches down to the ground, and when I sit it reaches to my ears; so I took my knife and cut one hair after another, and tied them together as I went down them. Meanwhile it grew dark, so I tied a knot in the hair, and resolved to rest on that knot through the night. But how should I do without a fire? The tinder-box I had by me, but I had no wood! Then I remembered I had somewhere in my overcoat a sewing-needle, so I found it, cut it in pieces and made a great fire, and when I was well warmed laid myself down near the fire to sleep. I slept soundly, but, unfortunately, a spark of fire burnt the hair through, and so head over heels I fell to the ground, and sank into the earth up to my girdle. I looked about to see how I could get out, and, seeing no help near, I hurried home for a spade and came back and dug myself out. Then I took the holy water to my father. When I arrived at home I found the reapers working in the corn-field. The corn was so high, that the reapers were almost burnt up. Then I shouted to them, "Why do you not bring our mare here which is two days' long and a day and a half broad, and on whose back large trees are growing? Bring her that she may make a little shadow on the field! My father quickly brought the mare, and the reapers worked on quite pleasantly in her shadow. Then I took a vessel to bring some water. But the water was frozen, so I took my head and broke the ice with it. Then I filled the vessel with water, and carried it to the reapers. When they saw me they all shouted, "But where is your head?" I put up my hand to feel for my head, and found, alas, that I had no head on my shoulders. I had forgotten it, and had left it by the water. So I returned quickly, but a fox had got there before me, and was drawing the brains from my head to eat. Then I approached slowly and struck the fox furiously, and he began to run, and, in running, dropped a little book from his pocket. I opened the book, and there I read, "The whole loaf is for me, and Beardless is to get nothing!"' So the boy caught up the loaf and ran off home, and Beardless remained looking after him.

THE WICKED STEPMOTHER.

THERE was once on a time a stepmother who hated her step-daughter exceedingly, because she was more beautiful than her own daughter whom she had brought with her into the house. By-and-by, the father learned also to hate his own child: he scolded her, and beat her, in order to please his wife. One day his wife said to him, 'Let us send your daughter away! Let her look out for herself in the world!' Upon this the man asked, 'Where can we send her? Where can the poor girl go alone?' To this the wife answered, 'If you will not do this, husband, I will no longer live with you. You had better take her to-morrow out of the house. You can lead her into the forest, and then steal away from her and hurry home!' She repeated this so often that at length he consented, but said, 'At least prepare the girl something for her journey, that she may not die the first day of hunger.'

The stepmother thereupon made a cake, and, the next morning early, the father led the girl far away into the very heart of the forest, and there left her and went back home.

The poor girl, thus left alone, wandered all day about the wood seeking for a path, but could find no way out of it. When it grew dark she got up into a tree to pass the night, fearing lest some wild beasts would eat her if she remained on the ground. And, indeed, all night long the wolves were howling under the tree, so that the poor girl trembled so much that she could hardly keep her herself from falling. When day dawned she descended from the tree and walked on again, hoping to find some way out of the forest. But the wood grew thicker and thicker, and seemed to have no end. In the evening whilst she was looking for a tree in which she might remain safely over the night, all at once she saw something shining in the forest. So she went on, hoping to find some shelter, and at length came to a fine large house. The gates were open, so she went in, and walked through a great many rooms, each one more beautiful than the other. On a table in one room she found a candle burning. She thought this must be the house of some robbers; but she was not afraid, for she reasoned with herself, 'Rich men have reason to fear robbers, but I have none—I will tell them that I will serve them gladly for a piece of bread?'

She then took the cake from her bag, said grace, and began to eat. Just as she had begun to eat a cock came into the room, and sprung upon the table to reach the cake, so the girl crumbled some of it for him. Then a little dog came in and jumped quite friendly upon her, so she broke a piece from her cake for the little dog, and took him on her knee, and petted and fed him. After that came in a cat also, and the girl fed her too.

At length the girl heard a loud noise as if some great beast was coming, and was greatly frightened when a lion came into the room. But the lion moved his tail in such a friendly way, and looked so very kindly, that she took heart, and offered him a piece of her cake. The lion took it and began to lick her hand, and the girl had no longer any fear of him, so she stroked him gently and fed him with the rest of the cake. Suddenly she heard a great noise of weapons, and almost swooned as a creature in a bear-skin entered the room. The cock, the dog, the cat, and the lion, all ran to it, and jumped about it affectionately, showing in all possible ways their great joy. The poor girl thought it a very strange beast, and expected it would jump upon her and kill her. But the fearful thing threw the bear-skin from its head and shoulders, and all the room shone and glittered with its golden garments. The poor girl almost lost her senses when she saw before her a handsome man, beautifully dressed. But he came up to her and said, 'Don't be afraid, my dear! I am not a bad man, I am the son of the king, and when I wish to hunt I come here and use this bear-skin as a disguise lest the people should recognise me. Those who see me believe that I am a ghost and run away from me. No one dares to come into this house, knowing that I often come here. You are the only person who has ventured in. How did you know that I am not a ghost?'

Then she told him she had never heard of him nor of the house, but that her stepmother had driven her away from home, and she told him all that had happened to her. When he heard this, he was very sorry, and said, 'Your stepmother hated you, but God has been kind to you. I will marry you if you are willing to be my wife—will you consent?' 'Yes!' she replied. Next day he took her to his father's palace and married her. After some time she begged to be allowed to go to see her father. So her husband allowed her to go, and she dressed herself all in gold and went to her father's house. The father happened to be away from home, and the stepmother, seeing her coming, was afraid lest she had come to revenge herself. So she hurried to meet her and said, 'You see that it was I who sent you on the road to happiness.' The step-daughter kissed her, and embraced her step-sister. Then the girl said she was very sorry that she had not found her father at home, and, on her going away, she gave plenty of money to her stepmother. When, however, she had gone away the stepmother shook her fist after her and cried, 'Wait a little, you shall not be the only one so dressed out; to-morrow I will send my own daughter after you the same way!'

When her husband came home at night she told him all that had happened, and said, 'What do you think, husband? would it not be a good thing to send my girl also into the wood to try her fortune; for your girl, whom we sent there, never came back until now, and now she has come glittering in gold?'

The man sighed and agreed to the proposal. Next day the stepmother prepared for her daughter plenty of cakes and roasted meats, and then sent her with the father into the forest. The man led her deep into the forest, as he had done his own daughter, and there left her. Finding the father did not return, she began to seek a way to get home, and soon came in sight of the house in the forest. She entered it, and seeing no one, fastened the door inside, saying as she did so, 'If God himself comes I will not open to Him.' Then she took out of her bag the baked meats and cakes and began to eat. Whilst she was eating, the cock, the dog, and the cat came in suddenly, and began to play about her affectionately, hoping she would give them something; but she became quite angry, and exclaimed, 'The devil take you! I have hardly enough for myself: do you think I will give any to you? Then she began to beat them; whereat the dog howled, and the lion hearing it rushed in furiously, caught the girl and killed her.

Next day the king's son came with his wife to hunt. She immediately recognised her sister's dress, and gathered together the fragments of the body, which she took to her stepmother. She found her father at home this time, and he was greatly pleased to hear that his daughter was married to the king's son. When, however, he heard what had happened with the daughter of his wife, he was very sorry, but said, 'Her mother has deserved this from the hand of God, because she hated you without a cause. There she is at the well, I will go and tell her.'

When the stepmother heard what had happened to her daughter, she said to her husband, 'I cannot bear your daughter! I cannot bear to look at her! Let us kill her and her husband. If you will not consent, I will jump down into this well!' 'I cannot kill my own child,' returned he. 'Well, then,' cried she, 'if *you* will not kill her, *I* cannot endure her!' and so she jumped down into the well.

BIRD GIRL.

ONCE upon a time lived a king, who had only one son; and when this son grew up, his father sent him to travel about the world, in order that he might find a maiden who would make him a suitable wife.

The king's son started on his journey, and travelled through the whole world without finding anywhere a maiden whom he loved well enough to marry. Seeing then that he had taken so much trouble, and had spent so much time and money, and all to no purpose, he resolved to kill himself. With this intention, he climbed to the top of a high mountain, that he might throw himself from its summit; for he wished that even his bones might never be found. Having arrived at the top of the mountain, he saw a sharp rock jutting out from one side of it, and was climbing up to throw himself from it, when he heard a voice behind him calling, 'Stop! stop! O man! Stop for the sake of three hundred and sixty-five which are in the year!' He looked back, and seeing no one, asked, 'Who are you that speak to me? Let me see you? When you know how miserable I am, you will not prevent me killing myself!'

He had scarcely said these words when there appeared to him an old man, with hair as white as wool, who said, 'I know all about you. But listen! Do you see that high hill?' 'Yes, I do,' said the prince. 'And do you see the multitude of marble blocks which are on it?' said the old man. 'Yes, I do,' rejoined the prince. 'Well, then,' continued the old man, 'on the summit of that hill there is an old woman with golden hair, who sits night and day on that very spot, and holds a bird in her bosom. Whoever can get this bird into his hands, will be the happiest man in the world. But, be careful. If you are willing to try and get the bird, you must take the old woman by her hair before she sees you. If she sees you before you catch her by her hair, you will be changed into a stone on the spot. Thus it happened to all those young men you see standing there, as if they were blocks of marble.'

When the king's son heard this, he thought, 'It is all one to me whether I die here or there. If I succeed, so much the better for me; if I fail, I can but die as I had resolved.' So he went up the hill. When he arrived near the old woman, he walked very cautiously towards her, hoping to reach her unseen; for, luckily, the old woman was lying with her back towards him, sunning herself, and playing with the bird.

When near enough, he sprang suddenly and caught her by the hair. Then the old woman cried out, so that the whole hill shook as with a great earthquake; but the king's son held fast by her hair, and when she found that she could not escape she said, 'What do you desire from me?' He replied, 'That you should give me the bird in your bosom, and that you call back to life all these Christian souls!' The old woman consented, and gave him the bird. Then from her mouth she breathed a blue wind towards the men of stone, and immediately they again became alive. The king's son, having the bird in his hands, was so rejoiced, that he began to kiss it; and, as he kissed it, the bird was transformed into a most beautiful maiden.

This girl the enchantress had turned into a bird, in order that she might allure the young men to her. The girl pleased the king's son exceedingly, and he took her with him, and prepared to return home. As he was going down the hill, the girl gave him a stick, and told him the stick would do everything that he desired of it. So the king's son struck with it once upon the rock, and in a moment there came out a mass of golden coin, of which they took plenty for use on their journey. As they were travelling they came to a great river, and could find no place by which they could pass over; so the king's son touched the surface of the river with his stick, and the water divided, so that a dry path lay before them, and they were able to cross over the river dryshod. A little farther they came to a herd of wolves, and the wolves attacked them, and seemed about to tear them to pieces; but the prince struck at them with his stick, and one by one the wolves were turned into ants. Thus, at length, the king's son reached home safely with his beloved, and they were shortly after married, and lived long and happily together.

SIR PEPPERCORN.

THREE brothers once upon a time went out into the neighbouring forest to choose some trees fit for building. Before going, however, they told their mother not to forget to send their sister into the wood after them with their dinners. The mother sent the girl as she had been told to do; but as the girl was on her way a giant met her in the wood, and carried her off to a cave, where he lived.

All day long the brothers waited, expecting their sister, and wondering why their mother had forgotten to send them food. At length, after remaining two days in the forest, and becoming anxious and angry at the delay, they went home. When they arrived there they asked their mother why she had not sent their sister with their food, as she had promised to do; she replied that she had sent the girl three days ago, and had been wondering greatly why she had not come back.

When the three brothers heard this they were exceedingly troubled, and the eldest said, 'I will go back into the forest and look for my sister.' Accordingly he went. After wandering about some time he came to a shepherdess, who was minding a flock of sheep.

He asked her anxiously if she had seen his sister in the wood, or whether she could tell him anything about her. The shepherdess replied that she had indeed seen a girl carrying food, but a giant had met her and carried her off to his cave. Then the young man asked her to tell him the way to the giant's cave; which she did. The cave was hidden in a deep ravine. The brother at once went down, and called aloud on his sister by name. In a short time the girl came to the mouth of the cave, and, seeing her eldest brother, invited him to come in. This he did, and was exceedingly surprised to see that the seeming cave was in reality a magnificent palace. Whilst he stood there, talking to his sister, and inquiring how she liked her new home, he heard a loud whirring in the air overhead, and, immediately afterwards, saw a heavy mace fall on the ground just in front of the cave. Greatly terrified and astonished, he asked his sister what this meant, and she told him not to be afraid, for it was only the way the giant let her know of his return three hours before he came, that she might begin to prepare his supper.

When it grew dark the giant came home, and was at once aware that a stranger was in his place. In reply to his angry questions, his wife told him it was 'only her brother, who had come to visit them.' When the giant heard this he went to the mouth of the cave, and calling a shepherd, ordered him to kill the largest sheep in his flock and roast it.

When the meat was ready the giant called his

brother-in-law, and said, as he cut the sheep in two equal parts, 'My dear brother-in-law, listen well to what I say; if you eat your half of the meat sooner than I eat mine, I will give you leave to kill me; but if I eat my half quicker than you eat yours, I shall certainly kill you.'

Thereupon the poor brother-in-law began to shake all over with fright; and, fearing the worst, tried to eat as fast as he could. But he had hardly swallowed three mouthfuls before the giant finished his share of the sheep, and killed him, according to his threat.

For some time the other two brothers and their old mother waited impatiently to see if the elder brother would come back. At last, hearing nothing either of the brother or of the sister, the second son said, 'I will go and look after them.' So he went into the same forest where his brother had gone, and, meeting there the same shepherdess minding her sheep, he inquired if he had seen his brother or sister. The shepherdess answered him as she had answered the elder brother, and he, too, asked the way to the giant's cave, and, on being told, went down the ravine until he reached the place. There he called on his sister by name, and she came out and invited him to enter the cave. This he did, and shared the fate of his brother; for, being unable to eat his part of the sheep as quickly as the giant ate his, he was also killed.

Not long after, the third brother went forth the same road, to look after his two elder brothers and sister, and, having found the giant's cave, was likewise invited to eat half a sheep, or be put to death. He, however, failed like his brothers had done before him, and being unable to eat his part of the sheep as quickly as the giant ate his, he was also killed.

Now the parents being alone in their house, prayed that God would give them another son, even were he no bigger than a peppercorn. As they prayed so it came to pass, and not very long after a little boy was born to them, who was so extremely small that they christened him 'Peppercorn.'

When the boy was old enough he went out to play with other boys; and one day, in a quarrel, one of these said to him, 'May you share the fate of your three elder brothers!' Hearing this, Peppercorn ran off home at once, and asked his mother what these words meant. So the mother was forced to tell him how his three brothers had gone into the forest to look after their lost sister, and had never come back again. As soon as he heard this, Peppercorn began to search the house for pieces of old iron, and, having found some scraps, carried them off in the evening to a blacksmith, that with them he might make him a mace. Next morning, Peppercorn went to the smith to ask for his mace, which the man gave him, saying at the same time, 'Now, pay me for making it.' To this, Peppercorn replied, 'First, let me see if it is strong enough:' and he threw it up in the air and held his head so that the mace might fall upon it. As soon as the mace struck his head, it broke into pieces; and Peppercorn, seeing how badly it was made, fell into a passion and killed the smith. Then he gathered up the pieces of iron, and went off to look for a better workman. He soon found another blacksmith who was willing to make him a mace, but demanded a ducat for the work. Peppercorn said he would willingly pay the ducat if the smith made him a really strong serviceable mace. So next morning he went to ask if it was ready, and the smith said 'Yes; but you must first pay me the ducat, and then I will give it you.' Peppercorn, however, answered, 'The ducat is ready in my pocket, but I must first see if the mace is good before I pay for it.' Thereupon he caught it, flung it up in the air, and held his head under it as it fell. As soon as the mace struck his head it broke into pieces; and he, again falling into a great passion, killed this smith also.

Gathering up the pieces of iron, he now carried them to a third smith, who undertook to make him a good strong mace, and demanded a ducat for doing so. Next morning Peppercorn went for the mace, and, after trying it three times, each time throwing it up higher in the air and letting it fall on his head, where it raised great bumps, he owned that he was satisfied with it, and accordingly paid the smith the ducat as he had promised.

Having now a good strong mace, Peppercorn started off at once for the forest, in which his three elder brothers and his sister had been lost. After wandering about for some time, he came to the place where the shepherdess sat watching her sheep, and, in reply to his questions, she told him that she had seen his three brothers go down the ravine in search of their sister, but had never seen them come up again.

Notwithstanding this, Peppercorn went resolutely down the ravine, calling aloud upon his sister by name. When she heard this she was exceedingly surprised, and said to herself, 'Who can this be calling me by name, now that all my brothers are killed? I have no other relations to come and look for me!' Then she went to the entrance of the cave and called out, 'Who is it that calls me; I have no longer any brothers?'

Peppercorn said to her, 'I am your brother who was born after you left home, and my name is Peppercorn!'

On hearing this, his sister led him into the palace, but he had hardly had time to say a few words to her before a loud whirring was heard in the air, and the giant's mace fell to the ground. For a moment Peppercorn was terrified at this, but he recovered himself quickly, and, pulling the mace out of the ground, flung it back to the giant, who, in astonishment, said to himself, 'Who is this who throws my mace back to me? Methinks I have at last found someone able to fight with me!'

When the giant came home, he immediately asked his wife who had been in the cave, and she answered him, 'It is my youngest brother!' Thereupon the giant ordered the shepherd to bring the largest sheep in his flock. When this was brought, the giant killed it himself, and, whilst preparing it for roasting, said to Peppercorn, 'Will you turn the meat, or will you take care of the fire?' Peppercorn said he would rather gather wood and make the fire; so he went out and tumbled down some large trees with his mace. These he carried to the mouth of the cave, and made a large fire ready for the meat.

When the sheep was roasted, the giant cut it in two parts, and gave one half to Peppercorn, saying, 'Take this half, and if you eat it before I eat my half you are free to kill me; but if you don't, I shall surely kill you!' So Peppercorn and the giant began to eat as fast as they could, swallowing down large pieces of meat, and, in their haste, almost choking themselves. At last, Peppercorn, by trickery, managed to get rid of his share of the sheep, and, according to the arrangement, killed the giant. This done, with the help of his sister, he collected all the treasures the giant had heaped up in his palace, and, taking them with him, returned home with his sister, to the great joy of their parents.

Peppercorn remained some time after this with his father, mother, and sister, and they lived very merrily on the treasures he had brought from the giant's cave. At length, however, he saw that the riches were coming to an end, so he resolved to go into the world to seek his fortune.

After travelling about a good while he came one day to a large city where he saw a great crowd gathered about a man who held an iron pike in his hand, and every now and then squeezed drops of water out of the iron. Whilst the people watched, wondering and admiring his great strength, Peppercorn went up and asked him, 'Do you think there is any man in the world stronger than yourself?'

'There is only one man alive who is stronger than myself, and that one is a certain person called Peppercorn,' answered he. 'Peppercorn can receive a mace on his head without being hurt!'

Thereupon Peppercorn told the man who he was, and proposed to him that they should travel about the world together.

'That will I right gladly,' said the Pikeman. 'How can I help being glad to go with a trusty fellow like you!'

Travelling together they came one day to a certain city, and, finding a concourse of people assembled, they went to see what was the matter. They found a man sitting on the bank of a river turning the wheels of nine mills with his little finger. So they said to him, 'Is there any one stronger than you in the world?'

And he answered them, 'There are only two men stronger than I am—a certain person named Peppercorn and a certain Pikeman.' Hearing this, Peppercorn and the Pikeman told him who they were, and proposed that he should join them in their travels about the world.

The Mill-turner very gladly accepted the offer, and so all three continued their journey together.

After travelling some time they came to a city where they found all the people greatly excited because some one had stolen the three daughters of the king, and, notwithstanding the immense rewards his majesty had offered, no one had as yet dared to go out to look for the princesses. As soon as Peppercorn and his two comrades heard this they went to the king and offered to search for his three daughters. But in order to accomplish the task they demanded that the king should give them a hundred thousand loads of wood. The king gave them what they wanted, and they made a fence all around the city with the timber. This done they began to watch.

The first morning they prepared a whole ox for their dinners, and discussed the question which of the three should stay behind to mind the meat whilst the other two watched the fence. The Pikeman said, 'I think I will stay here and take care of the meat, and I will have dinner ready for you when you come back from looking after the fence.' So it was thus settled. Just, however, as the Pikeman thought the ox was well roasted he was frightened by the sudden approach of a man with a forehead a yard high and a beard a span long. This man said to the Pikeman, 'Good morning!' but the latter ran away instead of answering, he was so shocked by the strange appearance of the man.

Yard-high-forehead-and-span-long-beard was quite content at this, and, sitting down, soon finished the whole ox. When he had ended his dinner he got up and went away.

Shortly afterwards Sir Peppercorn and the Millturner came for their dinners, and, being very hungry, shouted from afar to the Pikeman, 'Let us dine at once!' But the Pikeman, keeping himself hidden among the bushes, called out to them, 'There is nothing left for us to eat! A little while ago Yard-high-forehead-and-span-long-beard came up and ate up the whole ox to the very last morsel! I was afraid of him, and so I did not say one word against it.'

Peppercorn and the Mill-turner reproached their companion bitterly for allowing all their dinner to be stolen without once trying to prevent it, and the Mill-turner said scornfully, 'Well, I will stop to-morrow and look after the meat, and Yard-high-forehead-and-span-long-beard may come if he likes!'

So the next day the Mill-turner stayed to roast the ox, and his two comrades went to look after the fence they had built round about the city.

Just before dinner-time Yard-high-forehead-and-span-long-beard came out of the forest and walked straight up to the ox, and stretched his hands out greedily to grasp it. The Mill-turner was so frightened by his strange appearance that he ran off as hard as he could to look for a place to hide in.

By-and-by Peppercorn and the Pikeman came for their dinners and asked angrily where the meat was. Whereupon the Mill-turner answered, 'There is no meat! It has all been eaten by that horrible Yard-high-forehead-and-span-long-beard, and his looks frightened me so that I dared not say a single word to him.'

It was no use complaining, so Peppercorn only said, 'To-morrow I will stay to mind the ox, and you two shall go and look after the fence. I will see if we are to remain the third day without dinner.'

The next morning the Pikeman and the Mill-turner went to see if all was right round about the city, and Peppercorn remained to roast the ox. Exactly as on the two former days, just before dinner was ready, Yard-high-forehead-and-span-long-beard made his appearance, and went up to seize the meat. But Peppercorn pushed him roughly back, saying, 'Two days I have been dinnerless on your account, but the third day I will not be so, as long as my head stands on my shoulders!'

Much astonished at his boldness, Yard-high-forehead-and-span-long-beard exclaimed, 'Take care you don't begin to quarrel with me. There is no one in all the world who can conquer me, except a fellow called Peppercorn!'

Peppercorn was very pleased to hear this, and, without more hesitation, sprang at once on Yard-high-forehead-and-span-long-beard, and, after some struggling, pulled him down to the earth and bound him. This done, he tied him fast to a tall pine-tree. Now the Pikeman and Mill-turner came up and were exceedingly glad to find their dinners safe. Just as they were in the middle of their dinners, however, Yard-high-forehead-and-span-long-beard, with a sudden jerk, pulled up the pine-tree by the roots and ran off with tree and all, making furrows in the earth with it just as if three ploughs had been passing over the ground.

Seeing him run off, the Pikeman and Mill-turner

jumped up quickly and ran after him, but Peppercorn called them back and told them to finish their dinners first, for there would be plenty of time to catch him after they had dined! So they all three went on eating, and when they had done they followed the furrows which Yard-high-forehead-and-span-long-beard had made in the ground. After a while they came to a deep dark hole in the earth, and when they had examined it all round and tried in vain on account of the darkness to look down into it, they returned to the king and asked him to give them a thousand miles of strong rope so that they could go down into the pit.

The king at once ordered his servants to give them what they required, and when they had got the great cable they went back to the hole. On the way, as they were going, they discussed which of the three should venture down first, and it was at last settled that the Pikeman should be let down. However, he made them solemnly promise him that they should pull him up again the instant he shook the rope.

He had been let down but a very little way before he shook the rope, and so they pulled him up as they had promised.

Then the Mill-turner said, 'Let *me* go down.' And so the other two lowered him, but in a moment or two he shook the rope violently; and so he, too, was pulled up.

Now Peppercorn grew angry, and exclaimed, 'I did not think you were such cowards as to be afraid of a dark hole! Now let *me* down!' So they let him down and down until his foot touched solid ground. Finding that he had reached the bottom, he looked round him, and saw that he stood just in the very middle of a most beautiful green plain—a plain so beautiful that it was a real pleasure to look on it.

At one end of the plain stood a large handsome palace, and Peppercorn went nearer to look at it. There, in the gardens, walking, he met two young girls, and asked them if they were not the daughters of the king? When they said that they were, he inquired what had become of the other sister; and the princesses told him that their youngest sister was in the palace very busy binding up the wounds that Yard-high-forehead-and-span-long-beard had lately received from a certain knight called Peppercorn.

Then Peppercorn told them who he was, and that he had come down on purpose to release them, and to take them back to the king, their father. On hearing this good news, the two princesses rejoiced greatly, and told Peppercorn where he would find Yard-high-forehead-and-span-long-beard and their youngest sister. But they warned him not to rush in on the giant, but rather to go softly, and first try to get hold of the sabre which hung on the wall over his bed, for this sabre possessed the wonderful power of killing a man when he was a whole day's journey from it.

Peppercorn took care to do as the princesses had told him. He stole very quietly into the room where Yard-high-forehead-and-span-long-beard was lying, and when he was near the bed he sprang up suddenly and seized the sword. The moment the wounded giant saw his sabre in the hands of Peppercorn he jumped up quickly and ran out of the palace. Peppercorn followed him some time before he remembered what the two princesses had told him of the wonderful properties of the sword, but as soon as he recollected this he made a sharp cut with it in the air, as if he were cutting off a man's head, and the moment he did so Yard-high-forehead-and-span-long-beard fell down dead.

Then Peppercorn went back to the palace, and, taking with him the three princesses, prepared to return to the upper world.

When he came to the place where the rope was hanging he took a large basket, and, placing the eldest princess in it, fastened it to the rope, then, giving her a note, in which he said that he sent her for the Pike-man, he made the signal agreed upon for the rope to be drawn up. So his comrades pulled up the rope, and when it came down again with the empty basket, Peppercorn sent up the second princess, after giving her a paper, in which he had written, 'This one is for the Mill-turner.'

When the rope descended the third time he sent up the youngest princess, who was by far the most beautiful of the three. He gave her a paper which said that this one he meant to keep for himself. Just as the Pikeman and the Mill-turner began to pull up the rope the princess gave Peppercorn a little box, saying, 'Open it when you have need of anything!'

Now, when the Pikeman and Mill-turner drew up the

youngest princess, and saw how very beautiful she was, they determined to leave Peppercorn down in the pit, and go back without delay to the king's palace, and there see which of them could get the youngest princess for his wife.

Peppercorn waited patiently some time for the rope to be let down that he might be drawn up but no rope appeared. At last he was obliged to own to himself that his two comrades had deceived and deserted him, and, seeing how useless it was to remain standing still any longer, he walked off without knowing where the road would take him. Walking on, after a long time, he came to the shore of a large lake, and heard a great noise of crying and shouting. Very soon a multitude of people, looking like a wedding party, made their appearance. After placing a young girl in bridal attire on the shore of the lake, the people left her there alone and went away.

Peppercorn, seeing the girl left by herself, and noticing how sad she looked, went up to her, and asked her why her friends had left her there, and why she was so sad? The girl answered, 'In this lake is a dragon who, every year, swallows up a young girl. It is now my turn; and our people have brought me as a bride to the dragon, and left me to be swallowed up.'

Peppercorn, on hearing this, asked her to let him rest near her a little, because he was very tired, but she answered, 'You had far better fly away, my good knight; if it is necessary that I should die, it is not needful that you should die also.'

But Peppercorn said to her, 'Don't trouble yourself about me only let me rest near you a little, for I am very tired. It will be time enough for me to run away when the dragon comes.' Having said this he sat down near the girl, and in a little while fell asleep. He had not slept long before the surface of the lake became agitated, and the water rose up in large waves; presently the dragon lifted its head, and swam straight to the shore where the girl sat, evidently intending to swallow her at once. The maiden cried bitterly, and a tear falling on Peppercorn's face, awakened him. He sprang up quickly, grasped his sword, and, smiting fiercely, with one stroke, cut off the dragon's head.

Then he took the girl by the hand, and led her back to the city, where he found that she was the only daughter of the king of that country. The king was overjoyed at hearing that the dragon was killed, and also at seeing his daughter brought back to him safe and sound. So he insisted that Peppercorn should marry the princess, which he did, and they all lived together very happily for a long time.

After a while, however, Peppercorn began to long greatly for the other world, and grew sadder and sadder every day. When his wife noticed this change in his appearance she asked him very often what ailed him, but he would not tell her for a long time, because he did not wish to trouble her. At last, however, he could keep his secret no longer, and confessed to the princess how much he longed to go back to the upper world. Though she was very sorry to hear this, she promised him that she herself would beg the king to let him go, since he so greatly wished it. This she did: and when the king objected, not wishing to lose so good a son-in-law, the princess said, 'Let him go; he has saved my life, and why should we keep him against his will? My three sons will still remain to comfort us!'

Then the king consented, saying, 'Very well; let it be as he wishes, since you have nothing to say against it. Tell your benefactor to go to the lake-shore, and to say to the giant-bird he will find there, that the king sends her his greetings, and desires her to take the bearer of them up to the other world.'

The princess returned to her husband and told him what her father had said, and then began to prepare some provisions for the journey. When these were ready, and the king had sent the letter for the bird, Peppercorn took a kind leave of his wife, and went down to the lake-shore, where he soon found the nest of the giant-bird and her little ones in it, though she herself was not there. So he sat down to wait under the tree where the nest was. As he sat there, he heard the little birds chirping very restlessly and anxiously. Then he saw that the lake was beginning to throw up high waves, and soon a monster came out of the water and made straight for the nest to swallow the young birds.

Peppercorn, however, did not stop long to think about the matter, but quickly drew his wonderful sword and killed the monster. It happened that the giant-bird was just coming back, and when she saw Peppercorn under the tree, she shrieked as she ran up to kill him, 'Now I have caught you—you who have been killing all my little ones for so many years! Now you shall pay me for it, for I will kill you!' But the little birds from their nest high in the tree, cried out to her, 'Don't do him any harm! he has saved us from being swallowed by a monster who came out of the lake to kill us.'

Meanwhile, Peppercorn went to her, and presented the king's letter. The giant-bird read it through carefully, and then said to him, 'Go home and kill twelve sheep. Fill their skins with water, and bring them here, together with the flesh of the sheep.'

Peppercorn went back to the king, who at once ordered that he should be supplied with the flesh of twelve sheep, as well as with twelve sheep-skins full of fresh water. With this provision Peppercorn returned to the shore of the lake.

Then the giant-bird placed the twelve skins full of water under her left wing, and the flesh of the twelve sheep, under her right, and took Peppercorn on her back. This done, she told him that he must watch well her movements, and when she turned her beak to the left side, he must give her water, and when she turned it to the right he must give her meat. After impressing these directions upon Peppercorn, the giant-bird rose with her triple load in the air, and flew straight up towards the other world. As she flew she turned, from time to time, her beak, now to the left and then to the right, and Peppercorn gave her water or meat, as she had directed him to do. At last, however, all the meat disappeared. So, when the giant-bird turned her beak once more to the right, Sir Peppercorn, having no more meat to give her, and fearing some evil might happen if he did not satisfy her, took out his knife, and, cutting a piece of flesh from the sole of his right foot, gave it to her.

But the bird knew by the taste that he had cut it from his own foot, so she did not swallow it, but hid it under her tongue, and held it there until she reached the other world.

Then she set Peppercorn down on the earth and told him to walk, and when he tried to do so he was forced to limp, because of the loss of part of his foot. When the giant-bird noticed this, she asked him, 'Why do you limp so?' To this Peppercorn answered, 'Oh, it is nothing! Do not trouble yourself about it!' But the bird told him to lift his right foot, and when he did so, she took the piece of flesh she had kept hidden under her tongue, and laid it on the place where he had cut it from. Then she tapped it two or three times with her beak to make it grow to the rest of the foot.

Peppercorn walked on some time before he remembered the little box which the youngest of the three daughters of the king had given him. Now, however, he opened it, and a bee and a fly flew out and asked him what he desired. He said, 'I want a good horse to carry me to the king's residence, and a decent suit of clothes to wear.' Next moment a suit of good clothes lay before him, and a handsome horse stood ready saddled for him to mount. Then he took the clothes, and, mounting the horse, rode off to the city where the king dwelt. Before entering the city, however, he opened his little box, and said to the fly and the bee, 'I do not want the horse any more at present.' Accordingly they took it with them into their little box.

Peppercorn went to live in the house of an old woman in the city. Next morning he heard the public crier shouting in the street, 'Is there any one bold enough to fight with the mighty Pikeman, the king's son-in-law?'

Peppercorn was very pleased to hear this challenge, and, opening his box without delay, told the bee and fly, who flew out to receive his orders, that he wanted at once a fine suit of clothes and a strong charger, so that he might go to fight with the Pikeman. The bee and fly instantly gave him what he required, and he dressed himself and rode off to the field, where he found the Pikeman proudly awaiting any one who might presume to accept his challenge.

So Peppercorn and the Pikeman fought, and before very long the first son-in-law of the king was slain. Then Peppercorn returned home quickly, and opening his box, bade the bee and fly take away the horse and the fine clothes.

The king sought everywhere for the stranger who had killed his son-in-law, but no one knew anything about him. So, after some days, the city crier went round again, proclaiming that the Mill-turner, the second son-in-law of the king, would fight any one who dared to meet him.

Peppercorn again let out his bee and his fly, and asked for a finer horse and handsomer clothes than the last. So they brought him a very gorgeous suit, and a most beautiful coal-black charger, and with these he went on the field to meet the Mill-turner. They fought, but Peppercorn soon killed the king's second son-in-law, and again went to his lodgings, where he ordered the bee and fly to take the horse and clothes with them into their little box.

Now, not only the king, but all his people were very much puzzled as to who the powerful knight could be, who had killed the two valiant sons-in-law of the king. So a strict search was made, and he was sought everywhere. But no one could tell anything about him; while such horses as he rode, and such clothes as he wore were not to be found in the whole kingdom.

Some time had passed since the king's sons-in-law had been killed, and people had begun to be a little quieter and had given up all hope of finding out who the stronger knight might be. Then Peppercorn wrote a letter to the king's youngest daughter, and sent it to her by the old woman in whose house he lived. In the letter he told the princess everything that had happened to him since he had sent up in the basket to his false comrades, and told her also that he himself had slain both of the traitors in fair fight.

The young princess, as soon as she had read the letter, quickly ran to her father and begged him to pardon Peppercorn. The king saw he could not justly deny her this favour, since the two men who had been killed had deceived and deserted their friend, without whose superior courage they would never have been themselves his sons-in-law, seeing that all the three princesses, but for Peppercorn, must have remained in the other world where Yard-high-forehead-and-span-long-beard had carried them.

So, after thinking all this over in his mind, the king told his daughter that he willingly forgave Peppercorn, and that she might invite him to the palace. This the princess did at once, and very soon after Peppercorn made his appearance before the king in splendid attire, and was received very kindly.

Not long afterwards, the marriage of Peppercorn with the beautiful princess, the king's youngest daughter, was celebrated with great rejoicings, and the king built them a fine house near his palace to live in.

There Peppercorn and his princess lived long and happily, and he never had any wish to wander again about the world.

BASH-CHALEK; OR, TRUE STEEL.

ONCE upon a time there was a king who had three sons and three daughters. At length old age overtook him, and the hour came for him to die. While dying he called to him his three sons and three daughters, and told his sons to let their sisters marry the very first men who came to ask them in marriage. 'Do this, or dread my curse!' said he, and soon after expired.

Some time after his death there came one night a great knocking at the gate; the whole palace shook, and outside was heard a great noise of squeaking, singing, and shouting, whilst lightnings played round the whole court of the palace. The people in the palace were very much frightened, so that they shook for fear, when all at once some one shouted from the outside, 'O princes! open the door!' Thereupon the king's eldest son said, 'Do not open!' The second son added, 'Do not open, for anything in the world!' But the youngest son said, 'I will open the door!' and he jumped up and opened it.

The moment he had opened the door something came in, but the brother could see nothing except a bright light in one part of the room; out of this light came these words: 'I have come to demand your eldest sister for wife, and I shall take her away this moment, without any delay; for I wait for nothing, neither will I come a second time to ask her! Therefore answer me quickly —will you give her or not?'

The eldest brother said, 'I will not give her. How can I give her when I cannot see you, and do not know who you are, nor whence you come? You come tonight for the first time, and wish to take her away instantly! Should I not know where I can visit my sister sometimes?'

The second said, 'I will not give my sister to-night to be taken away!'

But the youngest said, 'I will give her if you will not. Have you forgotten what our father commanded us?' and, with these words, taking his sister by the hand, he gave her away, saying, 'May she be to you a happy and honest wife!'

As the sister passed over the threshold every one in the palace fell to the ground from fear, so vivid was the lightning and loud the claps of thunder. The heavens seemed to be on fire and the whole sky rumbled, so that the whole palace shook as if about to fall. All this however passed over, and soon after the day dawned; when it grew light enough, the brothers went to see if any trace was left of the mighty power, to whom they had given their sister, so that they might be able to trace the road by which it had gone. There was, however, nothing which they could either see or hear.

The second night, about the same time, there was

heard again round the whole palace a great noise, as if an army was whistling and hissing, and at length some one at the door cried out, 'Open the door, O princes!' They were afraid to disobey, and opened the door, and some dreadful power began to speak, 'Give here the girl, your second sister! I am come to demand her!' The eldest brother answered, 'I will not give her away!' The second brother said, 'I will not give you my sister!' But the youngest said, 'I will give her! Have you forgotten what our father told us to do?' So he took his sister by the hand and gave her over, saying, 'Take her! may she be honest and bring you happiness!' Then the unseen noises departed with the girl. Next day, as soon as it dawned, all three brothers walked round the palace, and for some distance beyond, looking everywhere for some trace where the power had gone, but nothing could be seen nor heard.

The third night, at the same hour as before, again the palace rocked from its very foundations, and there was a mighty uproar outside. Then a voice shouted, 'Open the door!' The sons of the king arose and opened the door, and a great power passed by them and said, 'I am come to demand your youngest sister!' The eldest and the second son shouted, 'No! we will not give our sister this third night! At any rate, we will know before our youngest sister goes away from our house to whom we are giving her, and where she is going, so that we can come to visit her whenever we wish to do so!' Thereupon the youngest brother said, 'Then I will give her! Have you forgotten what our father on his death-bed recommended us? It is not so very long ago!' Then he took the girl by the hand and said, 'Here she is! Take her! and may she bring you happiness and be happy herself!' Then instantly the power went away with a great noise. When the day dawned the brothers were very anxious about the fate of their sister, but could find no trace of the way in which she had gone.

Some time after the brothers, speaking together, said, 'Good God! it is really very wonderful what has happened to our sisters! We have no news—no trace of them! We do not know where they are gone, nor whom they have married!' At last they said to each other, 'Let us go and try to find our sisters!' So they prepared immediately for their journey, took money for their travelling expenses, and went away in search of their three sisters.

They had travelled some time when they lost their way in a forest, and wandered about a whole day. When it grew dark they thought they would stop for the night at some place where they could find water. So, having come to a lake, they decided to sleep near it, and sat down to take some supper. When the time for sleep came the eldest brother said, 'I will keep watch while you sleep!' and so the two younger brothers went to sleep and the eldest watched. In the middle of the night the lake began to be greatly agitated, and the brother who was watching grew quite frightened, especially when he saw something was coming towards him from the middle of the lake. When it came near he saw that it was a terrific alligator with two ears, and it ran at him; but he drew his knife and struck it, and cut off its head. When he had done this he cut off the ears also, and put them in his pocket, the body and the head, however, he threw back into the lake. Meanwhile the day began to dawn, but the two brothers slept on and knew nothing of what their eldest brother had done. At length he awakened them, but told them nothing, so they went on their travels together. When the next day was closing, and it began again to grow dark, they took counsel with each other where they should rest for the night, and where they should find water. They felt also afraid, because they were approaching some dangerous mountains.

Coming to a small lake they resolved to rest there that night; and having made a fire they placed their things near it, and prepared to sleep. Then the second brother said, 'This night I will keep guard whilst you sleep!' So the two others fell asleep, and the second brother remained watching.

All at once the lake began to move, and lo! an alligator, with two heads, came running to swallow up the three. But the brother who watched grasped his knife, felled the alligator to the ground with one blow, and cut off both the heads. Having done this he cut off the two pairs of ears, put them in his pocket, and threw the body into the water, and the two heads after it. The other brothers, however, knew nothing about the danger which they had escaped, and continued to sleep very soundly till the morning dawned.

Then the second brother awoke them, saying, 'Arise, my brothers! It is day!' and they instantly jumped up, and prepared to continue their journey. But they knew not in what country they now were, and as they had eaten up nearly all their food, they feared greatly lest they should die of hunger in that unknown land. So they prayed God to give them sight of some city or village or, at least, that they might meet some one to guide them, for they had already been wandering three days up and down in a wilderness, and could see no end to it. Pretty early in the morning they came to a large lake and resolved to go no further, but remain there all the day, and also to spend the night there. 'For if we go on,' said they, 'we are not sure that we shall find any more water near which we can rest.' So they remained there.

When evening came they made a great fire, took their frugal supper, and prepared to sleep. Then the youngest brother said, 'This night I will keep guard whilst you sleep;' and so the other two went to sleep, and the youngest brother kept awake, looking sharply about him, his eyes being turned often towards the lake. Part of the night had already passed, when suddenly the whole lake began to move, the waves dashed over the fire and half quenched it. Then he drew his sword and placed himself near the fire, as there appeared a great alligator with three heads, which rushed upon the brothers as if about to swallow them all three.

But the youngest brother had a brave heart, and would not awaken his brothers, so he met the alligator, and gave him three blows in succession, and at each blow he cut off one of the three heads. Then he cut off the six ears and put them in his pocket, and threw the body and the three heads into the lake. Whilst he was thus busy the fire had quite gone out, so he—having nothing there with which he could light the fire, and not wishing to awaken his brothers from their deep slumbers—stepped a little way into the forest, with the hope of seeing something with which he might rekindle the fire.

There was, however, no trace of any fire anywhere. At last, in his search, he climbed up a very high tree, and, having reached the top, looked about on all sides. After much looking he thought he saw the glare of a fire not very far off. So he came down from the tree and went in the direction in which he had seen the fire, in order to get some brand with which he might again light the fire. He walked very far on this errand, and though the glare seemed always near him, it was a very long time before he reached it. Suddenly, however, he came upon a cave, and in the cave a great fire was burning. Round it sat nine giants, and two men were being roasted, one on each side of the fire. Besides that, there stood upon the fire a great kettle full of the limbs of men ready to be cooked. When the king's son saw that, he was terrified and would gladly have gone back, but it was no longer possible.

Then he shouted as loud and cheerfully as he could, 'Good evening, my dear comrades! I have been a very long time in search of you!'

They received him well, saying, 'Welcome! if thou art of our company!'

He answered, 'I shall remain yours for ever, and would give my life for your sake!'

'Eh!' said they, 'if you intend to be one of us, you know, you must also eat man's flesh, and go out with us in search of prey?'

The king's son answered, 'Certainly; I shall do everything that you do!'

'Then come and sit with us!' cried the giants; and the whole company, sitting round the fire, took meat out of the kettle and began to eat. The king's son pretended to eat, also, but instead of eating he always threw the meat behind him, and thus deceived them.

When they had eaten up the whole of the roasted meat, the giants got up and said, 'Let us now go to hunt, that we may have meat for to-morrow.' So they went away, all nine of them, the king's son making the tenth. 'Come along!' they said to him, 'there is a city near in which a great king lives. We have been supplying ourselves with food from that city a great many years.' As they came near the city they pulled two tall pine-trees up by the roots, and carried them along with them. Having come to the city wall, they reared one pine-tree up against it, and said to the king's son, 'Go up, now, to the top of the wall, so that we may be able to give you the other pine-tree, which you must take by the top and throw down into the city. Take care, however,' they said, 'to keep the top of the tree in your hands, so that we can go down the stem of it into the city.' Thereupon the king's son climbed up on the wall and then cried out to them, 'I don't know what to do; I am not acquainted with this place, and I don't understand how to throw the tree over the wall; please one of you come up and show me what I must do.' Then one of the giants climbed up the tree placed against the wall, caught the top of the other pine-tree, and threw it over the wall, keeping the top all the time safe in his hand. Whilst he was thus standing, the king's son drew his sword, struck him on the neck, and cut his head off, so that the giant fell down into the city.

Then he called to the other eight giants, 'Your brother is in the city; come, one after the other, so that I can let you also down into the city!' And the giants, not knowing what had happened to the first one, climbed up one after the other, and thus the king's son cut off their heads till he had killed all the nine.

After that, he himself slowly descended the pine-tree and went into the city, walking through all the streets, but there was not one living creature to be seen. The city seemed quite deserted. Then he said to himself, 'Surely those giants have made this great devastation and carried all the people away.'

After walking about a very long time, he came to a tall tower, and, looking up, he saw a light in one of the rooms. So he opened the door, and went up the steps, into the room. And what a beautiful room it was in which he had entered! It was decorated with gold and silk and velvet, and there was no one there except a girl lying on a couch, sleeping. As soon as the king's son entered, his eyes fell upon the girl, who was exceedingly beautiful. Just then he saw a large serpent coming down the wall, and it had stretched out its head and was ready to strike the girl on the forehead, between the eyes. So he drew his dagger very quickly, and nailed the snake's head to the wall, exclaiming, 'God grant that my dagger may not be taken out of the wall by any hand but my own!' and thereupon he hurried away, and passed over the city wall, climbing up and going down the pine-trees. When he got back to the cavern where the giants had been, he plucked a brand from the fire, and ran away very quickly to the spot where he had left his two brothers, and found them still sleeping.

He soon lighted the fire again, and meanwhile the sun having arisen he awoke his brothers, and they arose and all three continued their journey. The same day they came to the road leading to the city. In that city lived a mighty king, who used to walk about the streets every morning, weeping over the great destruction of his people by the giants. The king feared greatly that one day his own daughter might also be eaten up by one of them. That morning he rose very early, and went to look about the city; the streets were all empty, because most of the people of the city had been eaten up by the giants. Walking about, at last he observed a tall pine-tree, pulled up quite by the roots, and leaning against the city wall. He drew near, and saw a great wonder. Nine giants, the frightful enemies of his people, were lying there with their heads off. When the king saw that he rejoiced exceedingly, and all the people who were left, gathered round and praised God, and prayed for good health and good luck to those who had killed the giants. At that moment a servant came running, to tell the king that a serpent had very nearly killed his daughter. So the king hurried back to the palace, and went quickly to the room wherein his daughter was, and there he saw the snake pinned to the wall, with a dagger through its head. He tried to draw the knife out, but he was not able to do so.

Then the king sent a proclamation to all the corners of the kingdom, announcing that whoever had killed the nine giants and nailed the snake to the wall, should come to the king, who would make him great presents and give him his daughter for a wife. This was proclaimed throughout the whole kingdom. The king ordered, moreover, that large inns should be built on all the principal roads, and that every traveller who passed by should be asked if he had ever heard of the man who had killed the nine giants, and any traveller who knew anything about the matter should come and tell what he knew to the king, when he should be well rewarded.

After some time the three brothers, travelling in search of their sisters, came one night to sleep at one of those inns. After supper the master of the inn came in to speak to them, and, after boasting very much what great things he had himself done, he asked them if they themselves had ever done any great thing?

Then the eldest brother began to speak, and said, 'After I started with my brothers on this journey, one night we stopped to sleep by a lake in the midst of a great forest; whilst my two brothers slept I watched, and, suddenly, an alligator came out of the lake to swallow us, but I took my knife and cut off its head; if you don't believe me, see! here are the two ears from his head!' And he took the ears from his pocket and threw them on the table.

When the second brother heard that, he said, 'I kept guard the second night, and I killed an alligator with two heads; if you do not believe me, look! here are its four ears!' and he took the ears out of his pocket and showed them.

But the youngest brother kept silence. The master of the inn began then to speak to him, saying, 'Well, my boy, your brothers are brave men; let us hear if you have not done some bold deed.'

Then the youngest brother began, 'I have also done something, though it may not be a great thing. When we stayed to rest the third night in the great wilderness on the shore of the lake, my brothers lay down to sleep, for it was my turn to keep guard. In the middle of the night the water stirred mightily, and a three-headed alligator came out and wished to swallow us, but I drew my sword and cut off all the three heads; if you do not believe, see! here are the six ears of the alligator!' The brothers themselves were greatly surprised, and he continued: 'Meanwhile the fire had gone out, and I went in search of fire. Wandering about the mountain I met nine giants in one cave;' and so he went on, telling all that had happened and what he had done.

When the innkeeper heard that he hurried off and told everything to the king. The king gave him plenty of money, and sent some of his men to bring the three brothers to him. When they came to the king, he asked the youngest, 'Have you really done all these wonders in this city—killed the giants and saved my daughter from death?' 'Yes, your majesty,' answered the king's son. Then the king gave him his daughter to wife, and allowed him to take the first place after him in the kingdom. After that he said to the two elder brothers, 'If you like I will also find wives for you two, and build palaces for you.' But they thanked him, saying they were already married, and so told him how they had left home to search for their sisters. When the king heard that, he kept by him only the youngest brother, his son-in-law, and gave the other two each a mule loaded with sacks full of money; and so the two elder brothers went back to their kingdom. All the time, however, the youngest brother was thinking of his three sisters, and many a time he wished to go in search of them again, though he was also sorry to leave his wife. The king would never consent to his going, so the prince wasted away slowly without speaking about his grief.

One day the king went out hunting, and said to his son-in-law, 'Remain here in the palace, and take these nine keys, and keep them carefully. If you wish, however,' added he, 'you can open three or four rooms, wherein you will see plenty of gold and silver, and other precious things. Indeed, if you much wish to do so, you can open eight of the rooms, but let nothing in the world tempt you to open the ninth. If you open that, woe to you!'

The king went away, leaving his son-in-law in the palace, who immediately began to open one room after another, till he had opened the whole eight, and he saw in all masses of all sorts of precious things. When he stood before the door of the ninth room, he said to himself, 'I have passed luckily through all kinds of adventures, and now I must not dare to open this door!' thereupon he opened it. And what did he see? In the room was a man, whose legs were bound in iron up to the knees, and his arms to the elbows; in the four corners of the chamber there were four columns, and from each an iron chain, and all the chains met in a ring round the man's neck. So fast was he bound that he could not move at all any way. In the front of him was a reservoir, and from it water was streaming through a golden pipe into a golden basin, just before him. Near him stood, also, a golden mug, all covered with precious stones. The man looked at the water and longed to drink, but he could not move to reach the cup. When the king's son saw that, he was greatly surprised, and stepped back; but the man cried, 'Come in, I conjure you in the name of the living God!' Then the prince again approached, and the man said, 'Do a good deed for the sake of the life hereafter. Give me a cup of water to drink, and be assured you will receive, as a recompense from me, another life.' The king's son thought, 'It is well, after all, to have two lives,' so he took the mug and filled it, and gave it to the man, who emptied it at once. Then the prince asked him, 'Now tell me, what is your name?' And the man answered, 'My name is True Steel.' The king's son moved to go away, but the man begged again, 'Give me yet one cup of water, and I will give you in addition a second life.' The prince said to himself, 'One life is mine already, and he offers to give me another—that is, indeed, wonderful!' So he took the mug and gave it to him, and the man drank it up. The prince began already to fasten the door, while the man called to him, 'Oh, my brave one, come back a moment! You have done two good deeds, do yet a third one, and I will give you a third life. Take the mug, fill it with water, and pour the water on my head, and for that I will give you a third life.' When the king's son heard that, he turned, filled the beaker with water, and poured it over the man's head, the moment the water met his head all the fastenings around the man's neck broke, all the iron chains burst asunder. True Steel jumped up like lightning, spread his wings, and started to fly, taking with him the king's daughter, the wife of his deliverer, with whom he disappeared. What was to be done now? The prince was afraid of the king's anger.

When the king returned from the chase, his son-in-law told him all that had happened, and the king was very sorry and said to him, 'Why did you do this? I told you not to open the ninth room!' The king's son answered, 'Don't be angry with me! I will go and find True Steel and bring my wife back!' Then the king attempted to persuade him not to go away: 'Do not go, for anything in the world!' he said; 'you do not know True Steel. It cost me very many soldiers and much money to catch him! Better remain here, and I will find you some other maiden for a wife; do not fear, for I love you as my own son, notwithstanding all that has happened!' The prince, however, would not hear of remaining there, so taking some money for his journey he saddled and bridled his horse, and started on his travels in search of True Steel.

After travelling a long time, he one day entered a strange city, and, as he was looking about, a girl called to him from a kiosk, 'O son of the king, dismount from your horse and come into the forecourt.' When he entered the courtyard the girl met him, and on looking at her he recognised his eldest sister. They greeted each other, and the sister said to him, 'Come, my brother—come with me into the kiosk.'

When they came into the kiosk, he asked her who her husband was, and she answered, 'I am married to the King of Dragons, who is also a dragon. I must hide you well, my dear brother, for my husband has often said that he would kill his brothers-in-law if he could only meet them. I will try him first, and if he will promise not to injure you, I will tell him you are here.' So she hid her brother and his horse as well as she could. At night, supper was prepared in readiness for her husband, and at last he came. When he came flying into the courtyard, the whole palace shone. The moment he came in, he called his wife and said, 'Wife, there is a smell of human bones here! Tell me directly what it is!'

'There is no one here!' said she. But he exclaimed, 'That is not true!'

Then his wife said, 'My dear, will you answer me truly what I am going to ask you? Would you do any harm to my brothers, if one of them came here to see me?' And the dragon answered, 'Your eldest and your second brother I would kill and roast, but I would do no harm to the youngest.' Then his wife said, 'Well, then, I will tell you that my youngest brother, and your brother-in-law, is here.' When the Dragon King heard that he said, 'Let him come to me!' So the sister led the brother before the king, her husband, and he embraced him. They kissed each other, and the king exclaimed: 'Welcome, brother-in-law!' 'I hope I find you well?' returned the prince courteously, and he told the Dragon King all his adventures from the beginning to the end.

Then the Dragon King cried out, 'And where are you going, my poor fellow? The day before yesterday True Steel passed here carrying away your wife. I assailed him with seven thousand dragons, yet could do him no harm. Leave the devil in peace; I will give you as much money as you like and then go home quietly.' But the king's son would not hear of going back, and proposed next morning to continue his journey. When the Dragon King saw that he could not change his intention, he took one of his feathers, and gave it into his hand, saying, 'Remember what I now say to you. Here you have one of my feathers, and if you find True Steel and are greatly pressed, burn this feather, and I will come in an instant to your help with all my forces.' The king's son took the feather and continued his journey.

After long travelling about the world he arrived at a great city, and, as he rode through the streets, a girl called to him from a kiosk: 'Here, son of the king! Dismount and come into the courtyard!' The prince led his horse into the yard, and behold! the second sister came to meet him. They embraced and kissed each other, and the sister led the brother up into the kiosk, and had his horse taken to a stable. When they were in the kiosk, the sister asked her brother how he came there, and he told her all his adventures. He then asked her who her husband was. 'I am married to the King of the Falcons,' she said, 'and he will come home to-night, so I must hide you somewhere, for he oftens threatens my brothers.'

Shortly after she had concealed her brother, the Falcon King came home. As soon as he alighted all the house shook. Immediately his supper was set before him, but he said to his wife, 'There are human bones somewhere!' The wife answered, 'No, my husband, there is nothing;' after long talking, however, she asked him, 'Would you harm my brothers if they came to see me?' The Falcon King answered, 'The eldest brother and the second I would delight in torturing, but to the youngest I would do no harm.'

So she told him about her brother. Then he ordered that they should bring him immediately; and when he saw him, he rose up and they embraced and kissed each other. 'Welcome, brother-in-law!' said the King of Falcons. 'I hope you are happy, brother?' returned the prince, and then they sat down to sup together. After supper, the Falcon King asked his brother-in-law where he was travelling. He replied that he was going in search of True Steel, and told the king all that had happened.

On hearing this the Falcon King began to advise him to go no farther. 'It is no use going on,' said he. 'I will tell you something of True Steel. The day he stole your wife, I assaulted him with four thousand falcons. We had a terrible battle with him, blood was shed till it reached the knees, but yet we could do him no harm! Do you think now, that you alone could do anything with him? I advise you to return home. Here is my treasure: take with you as much as you like.' But the king's son answered, 'I thank you for all your kindness, but I cannot return. I shall go at all events in search of True Steel!' For he thought to himself, 'Why should I not go, seeing I have three lives?' When the Falcon King saw that he could not persuade him to go back, he took a little feather and gave it him, saying, 'Take this feather, and when you find yourself in great need, burn it and I will instantly come with all my powers to help you!' So the king's son took the feather and continued his journey, hoping to find True Steel.

After travelling for a long time about the world he came to a third city. As he entered, a girl called to him from a kiosk, 'Dismount, and come into the courtyard.' The king's son went into the yard, and was surprised to find his youngest sister, who came to meet him. When they had embraced and kissed each other, the sister led her brother to the kiosk and sent his horse to the stables. The brother asked her, 'Dear sister, whom have you married? What is your husband?' She answered, 'My husband is the King of Eagles.' When the Eagle King returned home in the evening his wife received him, but he exclaimed immediately, 'What man has come into my palace? Tell me the truth instantly!' She answered, 'No one is here;' and they began their supper. By-and-by the wife said, 'Tell me truly: would you do any harm to my brothers if they came here?' The Eagle King answered, 'The eldest and second brother I would kill, but to the youngest I would do no harm! I would help him whenever I could!' Then the wife said, 'My youngest brother, and your brother-in-law, is here; he came to see me.' The Eagle King ordered that they should bring the prince instantly, received him standing, kissed him, and said, 'Welcome, brother-in-law!' and the king's son answered, 'I hope you are well?' They then sat down to their supper. During the repast they conversed about many things, and at last the prince told the king he was travelling in search of True Steel. When the Eagle King heard that, he tried to dissuade him from going on, adding, 'Leave the devil in peace, my brother-in-law; give up that journey and stay with me! I will do everything to satisfy you!' The king's son however, would not hear of remaining, but next day, as soon as it dawned, prepared to set out in search of True Steel. Then the Eagle King, seeing that he could not persuade him to give up his journey, plucked out one of his feathers and gave it him, saying, 'If you find yourself in great danger, my brother, make a fire and burn this feather; I will then come to your help immediately with all my eagles.' So the prince took the feather and went away.

After travelling for a very long time about the world, roaming from one city to another, and always going farther and farther from his home, he found his wife in a cavern.

When the wife saw him she was greatly astonished, and cried, 'In God's name, my husband, how did you come here?' He told her how it all happened, and then added, 'Now let us fly!' 'How can we fly,' she asked, 'when True Steel will reach us instantly? and when he does he will kill you, and carry me back.' But the prince, knowing he had three other lives to live, persuaded his wife to flee, and so they did. As soon, however, as they started, True Steel heard it, and followed immediately. When he reached them, he shouted to the king's son, 'So, prince, you have stolen your wife!' Then, after taking the wife back, he added, 'Now, I forgive you this life, because I recollect that I promised to give you three lives; but go away directly, and never come here again after your wife, else you will be lost!' Thus saying, he carried the wife away, and the prince remained alone on the spot, not knowing what to do.

At length the prince resolved to go back to his wife. When he came near the cave he found an opportunity when True Steel was absent, and took his wife again and tried to escape with her.

But True Steel learned their flight directly, and ran after them. When he reached them, he fixed an arrow to his bow, and cried to the king's son, 'Do you prefer to die by the arrow or by the sword?' The king's son asked pardon, and True Steel said, 'I pardon you also the second life; but I warn you! never come here again after your wife, for I will not pardon you any more! I shall kill you on the spot!' Saying that, he carried the wife back to the cave, and the prince remained thinking all the time how he could save her.

At last he said to himself, 'Why should I fear True Steel, when I have yet two lives? One of which he has made me a present, and one which is my own?' So he decided to return again to the cave next morning, when True Steel was absent. He saw his wife, and said to her, 'Let us fly!' She objected, saying, 'It is of no use to fly, when True Steel would certainly overtake us.' However, her husband forced her to go with him, and they went away. True Steel, however, overtook them quickly, and shouted, 'Wait a bit! This time I will not pardon you!' The prince became afraid, and begged him to pardon him also this time, and True Steel said to him, 'You know I promised to give you three lives, so now I give you this one, but it is the third and last.' Now you have only one life, so go home, and do not risk losing the one life God gave you!'

Then the prince, seeing he could do nothing against this great power, turned back, reflecting, however, all the time, as to the best way of getting his wife back from True Steel.

At last, he remembered what his brothers-in-law had said to him when they gave him their feathers. Then he said to himself, 'I will try this fourth time to get my wife back; if I come to trouble, I will burn the feathers, and see if my brothers-in-law will come to help me.'

Hereupon he went back once more towards the cavern wherein his wife was kept, and, as he saw from a distance that True Steel was just leaving the cave, he went near and showed himself to his wife. She was surprised and terrified, and exclaimed, 'Are you so tired of your life that you come back again to me?' Then he told her about his brothers-in-law, and how each of them had given him one of their feathers, and had promised to come to help him whenever he needed their assistance. 'Therefore,' added he, 'I am come once more to take you away; let us start at once.'

This they did. The same moment, however, True Steel heard of it, and shouted from afar, 'Stop, prince! You cannot run away!' And then the king's son, seeing True Steel so near him, quickly took out a flint and tinder-box, struck some sparks, and burned all three feathers. Whilst he was doing this, however, True Steel reached him, and, with his sword, cut the prince in two parts. That moment came the King of Dragons, rushing with his whole army of dragons, the King of Falcons, with all his falcons, and the King of Eagles, with his mighty host of eagles, and they all attacked True Steel. Torrents of blood were shed, but after all True Steel caught up the woman and fled away.

Then the three kings gave all their attention to their brother-in-law, and determined to bring him back to life. Thereupon they asked three of the most active dragons which of them could bring them, in the shortest time, some water from the river Jordan.

One said, 'I could bring it in half an hour.' The second said, 'I can go and return in ten minutes.' The third dragon said, 'I can bring it in nine seconds.' Then the three kings said to the last one, 'Go, dragon; and make haste!' Then this dragon exhibited all his fiery might, and in nine seconds, as he had promised, he came back with water from the Jordan.

The kings took the water and poured it on the places where the prince was wounded, and, as they did so, the wound closed up, the body joined together, and the king's son sprang up alive.

Then the three kings counselled him: 'Now, that you are saved from death, go home!' But the prince answered, he would at all events yet once more try to get his wife back. The kings, his brothers-in-law, again spoke, 'Do not try again! Indeed, you will be lost if you go, for now you have only one life which God gave you!'

The king's son, however, would not listen to their advice. So the kings told him, 'Well then, if you are still determined to go, at least do not take your wife away immediately, but tell her to ask True Steel where his strength lies, and then come and tell us, in order that we may help you to conquer him!'

So the prince went secretly and saw his wife, and told her how she could persuade True Steel to tell her where his strength was. He then left her and went away.

When True Steel came home, the wife of the king's son asked him, 'Tell me, now, where is your great strength?' He answered, 'My wife, my strength is in my sword!' Then she began to pray, and turned to his sword. When True Steel saw that, he burst out laughing, and said, 'O foolish woman! my strength is not in my sword, but in my bow and arrows!' Then she turned towards the bow and arrows and prayed.

Then True Steel said, 'I see, my wife, you have a clever teacher who has taught you to find out where my strength lies! I could almost say that your husband is living, and it is he who teaches you!'

But she assured him that no one taught her, for she had no longer any one to do so.

After some days her husband came, and when she told him she could not learn anything from True Steel, he said, 'Try again!' and went away.

When True Steel came home she began again to ask him the secret of his strength. Then he answered her,

'Since you think so much of my strength, I will tell you truly where it is.' And he continued, 'Far away from this place there is a very high mountain; in the mountain there is a fox; in the fox there is a heart; in the heart there is a bird, and in this bird is my strength. It is no easy task, however, to catch that fox, for she can transform herself into a multitude of creatures.'

Next day, as soon as True Steel left the cave, the king's son came to his wife, and she told him all she had learned. Then the prince hurried away to his brothers-in-law, who waited, all three impatient to see him, and to hear where was the strength of True Steel. When they heard, all three went away at once with the prince to find the mountain. Having got there, they set the eagles to chase the fox, but the fox ran to a lake, which was in the midst of the mountain, and changed herself into a six-winged golden bird. Then the falcons pursued her, and drove her out of the lake, and she flew into the clouds, but there the dragons hurried after her. So she changed herself again into a fox, and began to run along the earth, but the rest of the eagles stopped her, surrounded, and caught her.

The three kings then ordered the fox to be killed, and her heart to be taken out. A great fire was made, and the bird was taken out of the heart and burnt. That very moment True Steel fell down dead, and the prince took his wife and returned home with her.

THE SHEPHERD AND THE KING'S DAUGHTER.

A LONG time ago there lived a poor woman who possessed nothing in the world except one son and four lambs. The boy took the lambs out to graze every morning, and brought them home every night. One day it happened that the lambs were grazing in a field not far from the summer palace of the king, and the king's daughter came out to the young shepherd and asked him to give her one of them. The boy refused, saying, 'I cannot give you one, for my mother will scold me if I do, as we have nothing in the world except these four lambs.' The princess, however, had taken so great a fancy for a lamb that she would not be refused, and at last said, 'Only let me have this one and I will give you any price you like to ask.'

The boy, seeing that the princess would not go away without a lamb, considered a little how he could get rid of her, and then he told her that he would give her one if she would show him one of her shoulders. To his great surprise the princess, without any hesitation, pushed her mantle aside and showed him her bare white arm, and he noticed that on the shoulder there was a mark like a star. He was obliged now to give her one of his lambs, and when he went home in the evening he told his mother that he had fallen asleep at noon, and that when he awoke, one of the lambs had vanished, and he could not find it anywhere.

Then his mother scolded him very much, saying, 'I see you will bring me to the beggar's staff with your carelessness! To-morrow you must take these three lambs out to graze very early, and look well about for the lost one. And if you don't find it you had better never let me set eyes on you again.'

At dawn the next day the boy took the three lambs to graze in the same field, and sat down to consider how he could get back the lamb he had lost. At noon, when no one was about, the king's daughter came out of the palace and said to him, 'Young shepherd, give me another lamb, and ask what you please in return.' But the boy answered, 'No! I dare not give you another; I have suffered enough for the one I gave you yesterday! So please go and bring me my lamb back.'

This the princess refused to do, and said, 'It is quite useless to speak of such a thing. But tell me, did you notice anything particular on my shoulder?'

The youth answered, 'Yes, I saw a star!'

'Ah!' exclaimed the princess; 'for that you can never pay me enough, and yet you want your lamb back!' So they almost quarrelled, for the king's daughter persisted in begging him to give her another lamb, and the young shepherd insisted that she should bring him the first one back again.

At last, seeing there was no end to her begging, the boy said, 'Well! I will give you one if you uncover before me your other shoulder.' This the princess did instantly, and he remarked that she had the mark of a star on that arm also. In this way he lost a second lamb; and when the evening came he went home very sadly, feeling sure his mother would scold him. And so she did, far more than at the first time, calling him ill names and threatening to beat him. The boy was really sorry that he had given way to the princess's prayers, but he could not help it now. Next day, again, the princess came to him and begged so hard and so long for a third lamb that he became impatient, and, thinking to shame her, said he would give her one if she showed him her neck. To his great surprise, however, the king's daughter at once let her mantle fall, and he saw that she had the mark of a crescent on her throat. So the poor boy lost a third lamb, and hardly dared go home to his mother at night with the one lamb left them. Indeed the poor old woman was so angry at her son's carelessness in losing one lamb after another whilst he slept—for he did not dare to tell her the truth about the princess—that she cursed him as "a good-for-nothing who would bring her to beggary.'

Notwithstanding all his mother's reproaches and threats the boy could not refuse the princess the next day when she came out to ask for the fourth lamb. However, he tried to get her to go away a long time, and not until quite tired out with her begging, did he exclaim, 'Well, I will give you the lamb if you will show me your breast!' Then the princess pushed her robe aside, and the boy noticed that she had the mark of a sun on her bosom.

In this way the young shepherd lost all the four lambs, and he lived a long time with his mother in great poverty.

A long, long time afterwards the king sent out a proclamation that he intended to let his daughter marry, and would give her to that man who could tell him what particular birth-marks she had about her. The young shepherd heard this proclamation, and when he went home in the evening he said to his mother, 'Mother, I intend to go to the king's palace to-morrow, so get me my best linen ready.'

'And what do *you* want in the king's palace?' asked the poor old woman wondering.

"I intend, God helping me, to marry the king's daughter,' replied the young man boldly.

'Oh! you had better give up that fancy,' cried the mother. 'It will be better for you to go and work and gain a piaster than to go, like a fly without a head, dreaming about things that are as high as the sky above you.'

But the young man would not be persuaded, and went the next day to the king's palace. Before going out of the hut, however, he said to his anxious old mother, 'Good-bye, mother.'

He had not walked very far before a gipsy met him, and asked, 'Where are you going, my young man?'

'I am going to the king's palace,' answered the

youth, 'and I mean, God helping me, to marry the king's daughter.'

'But, my dear comrade,' said the gipsy, keeping near him, 'how can you really expect that she will marry you, when you are so poor? Only a shepherd!'

'Eh!' returned the young man; 'but I know what birth-marks she has, and the king has sent out a proclamation that whoever guesses these shall have her for his wife.'

'If it is so,' rejoined the cunning gipsy, 'I myself will also go to the palace with you.'

The young man was glad to have company on the road, and so he and the gipsy travelled on together until they came to the residence of the king.

When they came to the palace they found a large number of people who had come to 'try their luck,' and guess what birth-marks the princess had. But it was lost time, for every one of them, after going past the king and guessing 'by good luck' at the marks of the princess, was obliged to go away, having lost his time and gained nothing. At length the turn came for the young shepherd to pass before the king, and the gipsy kept close to him to hear what he would say.

So the youth stepped before the king and said, 'The princess has a star on each shoulder, and a crescent on the throat——'

At this moment the gipsy shouted loudly, 'Look there! that is just what I was going to say!'

'Be quiet!' said the young shepherd; 'or, if you really know what other marks she has, speak out.'

'No, no!' cried the gipsy, 'go on, go on! When *you* have done, *I* will speak what I know!'

Then the youth turned again to the king and continued, 'The princess has the mark of a sun on her bosom ——'

'That is exactly what I was going to say!' cried the gipsy, coming up quickly; 'she has the mark of a sun on her breast.'

Now the king was exceeding surprised, and confessed to his counsellors that the young shepherd had really guessed the truth. But as neither the king nor the counsellors at all liked the idea of the princess marrying a poor shepherd, they consulted how they could get rid of him without giving the lie to the king's proclamation. At length it was decided that his Majesty should say, 'As both the shepherd and the gipsy have guessed the princess's birth-marks, I cannot justly decide which of them should marry her. But I will give to each of them seventy piasters, and they must both go and trade with this money for a year. At the end of the year, that one which brings back the most money shall have the princess for his wife.'

The young shepherd and the gipsy, having received the money, went off in opposite directions to seek their fortunes.

After having travelled about some time, like a fly without a head, not knowing where — the shepherd stopped one night to rest in the hut of an old woman, who was even poorer than his own mother.

As he sat with the old woman in the hut that evening,

the lad thought he might just as well ask her advice as to the best way to invest his capital of seventy piasters, so he said : 'I have seventy piasters to trade with, can you tell me some good way in which I may employ them profitably?'

The old woman considered the matter for some time before she answered, and then said, 'To-morrow is market-day in the next city; go there yourself, and when a man brings a very poor cow for sale, go up and try to buy it. The cow will be of many different colours, but very thin and ill fed, but you must buy her at whatever price the man asks for her. When you have bought her, bring her here at once.'

The young man agreed to follow the old woman's counsel, and so next day he went to the city and really found there a man who had brought a poor, but variously coloured, cow to sell. Many people wished to buy the cow, but the young man outbid them all, and at length offered all his seventy piasters for her. So he got the cow, and drove it to the hut where he had passed the night. When the old woman came out to see who was coming, he called out to her, 'Now, my old mother, I have bought the cow, and what shall we do with her? She has cost me all my capital!'

The old woman answered at once, 'Kill the cow, my son, and cut it in pieces.'

'But how will that bring me back my money with profit?' asked the young shepherd, hesitating whether he should follow her advice or no.

'Don't be afraid, my son, but do as I say,' returned the old woman. Accordingly he did as she advised him, killed the cow and cut her into pieces. This done, he asked again, 'And now, what shall I do?' The old woman said quietly, 'Well, now we will eat the meat, and the suet we will melt down and put into a pot to keep for some other occasion.'

The shepherd did not at all like this proposal, for he could not see what return he could hope to get for such an investment of his capital. However, he thought within himself, 'Well, since I have been foolish enough to follow her counsel on the two former occasions, I may as well follow it also this third time.' So he remained with the old woman many days, until the last piece of meat had been eaten up. When, however, he thought over all that had happened, he grew very sad, and, seeing no sign of anything better, said one morning to the old woman reproachfully, 'Now you see by following your counsel I have spent all the king's money, and am now a ruined man!'

'Don't be afraid, my son,' said the old woman; 'you can now take that pot of suet with you and go to the black world, where all the people are black as chimney-pots, and there you can sell for a good deal of money your suet, for it has the power to make the black skin white.'

The poor shepherd was very glad at hearing this, and next morning took the pot of suet on his shoulder and started on his journey. After he had travelled many, many days, he came to a strange-looking country, and, going a little farther, he saw a man who was quite black, just as the old woman had said—as black as a chimney-pot. He was immediately going to offer to sell some of his fat to the black man, when the latter, frightened at the sight of a white man, ran away. Many other black men who saw him did the same, but after a while, when they saw that he went on quietly carrying his pot on his shoulder, they took courage, and came to him one by one, until at last quite a large crowd had gathered about him. At length, one of them ventured to say to him, 'You strange-looking man, tell us who you are, and where you come from, and why did you come here?' The shepherd answered, 'I am a white man from a white world, and I come to bring you some fat which will make you also white—that is, of course, if you choose to buy it from me and pay me for it well.'

Now the black men, though they had been quite shocked at first to see the white man, began to think they also would like to be white; so they said they were willing to pay him as much as he liked to ask for his wonderful fat, because they were very rich.

However, they doubted a little if the fat would really make them white as he said, and wished to see it tried before they bought it. Thereupon he set the pot on the ground, and walked round and round it, saying some queer words as if he were charming it. Then he took out of the pot a little of the fat, and with it smeared one of the black men. In a moment the black skin became quite white, and the other blacks, seeing that he had told them the truth, crowded eagerly round him, begging that he would make them white also, and outbidding each other in offers of money, provided only that he made them white in a short time. The young shepherd worked hard, smearing one black skin after the other, until he got quite weary and had become very rich, for they gave him a good deal of money, and there were a great many of them who wished to be made white.

Just as he had thus whitened the last of the black men about him, one of them said to him, 'Wonder-working man! We have a king who, being our chief, is the blackest of us all; therefore, if you think you can make him white also, we are sure he will be very glad to get rid of his blackness, and will pay you more money than you ever dreamt of.'

'I will do it very gladly,' answered the shepherd; 'for you must know I am doing this not so much for the sake of money as for charity; only, show me at once the way to your king.'

So they all ran off before him to show him the way, and he followed them carrying his pot on his shoulder.

When they arrived at the door of the king's palace, one of the men said to him, 'Wait a moment here, whilst I go and tell his Majesty all about your wonderful fat, and ask him to receive you.' The shepherd waited quietly, though crowds gathered round him to stare at him and his great pot, until the man came back and said the king was waiting impatiently to see him. So he lifted his pot again on his shoulder—for he had set it down that he might rest the better—and followed the messenger to the king's presence.

Now the king of the black men was far blacker than anything the shepherd had ever seen in his life; he had no doubt, however, after all he had seen, but that his fat would whiten him also. So he said cheerfully, 'Good morning, your Majesty!' 'Good morning, my dear fellow,' returned the black king; 'I have heard that you can do wonders, and I have seen that you have already whitened many of my subjects, so, for Heaven's sake, deliver me also from this my blackness, and ask in return whatever you like, even the half of my kingdom!'

'What your Majesty has heard is quite true,' said the shepherd; 'and I will very gladly try to make you also white!' and he took a great lump of fat and rubbed it well all over the king's face and neck. In a moment the king became as white as snow, to the great rejoicings of all his people. But no one was so pleased as the king himself, so he said again, 'Only ask! I will give you whatever you wish, even if it be my throne!'

'I thank your Majesty very humbly for offering me your throne, but I don't want it,' replied the shepherd; 'but if you will give me three ships full of gold and silver, and some good sailors to manage the ships, and some good soldiers and cannons to defend them against the pirates, I shall think myself more than repaid, and I will send you back the ships and cannons when the gold and silver are landed safely in my country.'

Then the king at once gave the necessary orders, and in a very few days his servants came to report to him, that the ships were then filled with gold and silver, and that the cannons were ready loaded and posted for action, and all the sailors and soldiers prepared to fight if any sea-robber came in their way.

Then the young shepherd took a courteous leave of the king, and of all those other people who were so thankful to him for having changed them from black men into white ones. He now went on board one of the ships, very glad to go back to his own country, and the two other ships full of gold and silver followed the first one across the seas.

After having sailed a long time the three ships reached at last the coast of the kingdom where the king was waiting, daily expecting the return of the gipsy and shepherd to claim his daughter. The shepherd let his ships lay quietly in the harbour one day, and then, noticing much tumult and disturbance in the city, went ashore to see what had happened. There he found a great crowd, and on asking some of the people what they were going to do, they told him that they were going to hang a gipsy who had come to the city with seventy piasters capital, and who had not only spent all his money in drinking and revellings, but had even got into debt for seventy other piasters, which he was quite unable to pay, and that this was the reason they were about to hang him. In a few moments the hangman appeared, leading the gipsy, who was no other than the very man who had tried to cheat the shepherd out of the princess.

The young shepherd recognised his rival at once, and, going near him, said, 'What is this, my old friend?

Have you really come to this?' The instant the gipsy saw the shepherd he stopped and began to whine and wail, begging him to save him from the gibbet, and he would be his faithful servant all his life. 'As for the princess,' he added cunningly, 'I have given her up a long time ago, and don't care for anything if only my life is spared.'

Then the young shepherd was sorry for the poor trembling, whining wretch, and offered to pay the debt for the gipsy if the people would let him off. So they agreed to this, and the young man not only paid the seventy piasters the gipsy owed, but bought him besides a suit of good clothes as well as a carriage and a pair of fine horses. Then he left him and went back to his ships, and they sailed on slowly along the coast towards the king's residence.

Now when the gipsy had dressed himself out smartly in his fine new clothes, he got into his carriage and drove off quickly to the king's palace. Arrived there, he left his carriage and horses in the courtyard, and went at once to the presence of the king, whom he addressed thus: 'Your Majesty knows it is not yet quite a year since you gave me seventy piasters to trade with, and see! I come back already handsomely dressed, and have a fine carriage with a pair of beautiful horses below in the yard. As for the young shepherd, I have heard that he has not only spent all your Majesty's money in rioting, but that he had also got in debt, for which he has been hung. So it is no use waiting for him! Let us keep my wedding at once!'

The king did not fancy the gipsy for his son-in-law, and was thinking what he could say to put him off a little time, when, looking by chance through his window, he saw three strange-looking ships sailing slowly towards the shore. At this he exclaimed, 'I see some foreign visitors are coming to visit me, and I shall have enough to do to receive them with due honours, so we must put off the marriage for some days, at least!'

But the gipsy pressed the king more and more to let him marry the princess at once; he was even bold enough to tell his Majesty that he could not wait any longer, and that the wedding would be all over in an hour. The king, however, refused to hear anything of this; so the gipsy, seeing that his plan had failed, went out from the presence of the king in great anger.

A few hours later the three strange-looking ships dropped their anchors just opposite the palace, and the young shepherd, landing, came into the presence of the king, who was greatly astonished to see him alive, and still more astonished to hear that in return for his seventy piasters he had brought three vessels full of gold and silver.

The king was now very well content to accept him as his son-in-law, and told him, in the course of conversation, what the gipsy had said about his having gone in debt and been hung. Then the young shepherd told his Majesty how he had found the gipsy, and had saved his life by paying his debt for him. The king was exceedingly angry, and ordered his servants to go after the gipsy and bring him at once into his presence.

The servants looked about and around the palace on all sides, but nowhere could they find any trace of the gipsy. Then the king commanded that some of them should go in search of him without delay, and armed men were speedily scattered over the whole country, so that at last he was caught, and brought before the king, who condemned him to be hung for having so shamefully tried to injure the man who had saved his life and treated him so generously, and for having, at the same time, attempted to cheat the king.

The young shepherd spent a few days in the palace, telling the king all the things he had seen in the black world, and then, all preparations having been made, he was married to the princess, with great pomp and rejoicings.

Then the king with his daughter and son-in-law lived for a great many years very happily.

ONE GOOD TURN DESERVES ANOTHER.

IT happened once upon a time, many years ago, that a certain king went into his forest to hunt, when instead of the usual game he caught a wild man. This wild man the king had taken to his castle, and locked up, for safety, in a dungeon. This done, he put out a proclamation that whosoever should dare to set the wild man free should be put to death.

As luck would have it, the dungeon where the creature was confined was just below the sleeping-room of the king's youngest son. Now the wild man cried and groaned incessantly to be set free, and these unceasing lamentations at length so moved the young prince that one night he went down and opened the dungeon door, and let out the prisoner.

Next morning the king and all the courtiers and servants were exceedingly astonished to hear no longer the usual sounds of wailing from the dungeon, and the king, suspecting something amiss, went down himself to see what had become of his captive. When he found the den empty he flew into a great passion, and demanded fiercely who had presumed to disobey his commands and let out the wild man. All the courtiers were so terrified at the sight of the king's angry countenance, that not one of them dared speak, not even to assert their innocence. However, the young prince, the king's son, went forward at last and confessed that the pitiful crying of the poor creature had so disturbed him day and night, that at length he himself had opened the door. When the king heard this, it was his turn to be sorry, for he found himself compelled to put his own son to death or give his own proclamation the lie.

However, some of his old counsellors, seeing how greatly the king was perplexed and troubled, came and assured his Majesty that the proclamation would in reality be carried out if the prince, instead of being put to death, was simply banished from the kingdom for ever.

The king was very glad to find this way of getting out of the dilemma, and so ordered his son to leave the country, and never come back to it, at the same time he gave him many letters of recommendation to the king of a very distant kingdom, and directed one of the court servants to go with the young prince to wait upon him. Then the unhappy young prince and his servant started on their long journey.

After travelling some time, the young prince became very thirsty, and, seeing a well not far off, went up to it to drink. However, there happened to be no bucket at the well, nor anything in which to draw water, though the well was pretty full. Seeing this, the young prince said to his servant, 'Hold me fast by the heels, and let me down into the pit that I may drink.' So saying, he bent over the well, and the servant let him down as he was directed.

When the prince had quenched his thirst, and wished to be pulled back, the servant refused, saying, 'Now I can let you fall into the pit in a moment, and I shall do so unless you consent at once to change clothes and places with me. I will be the prince henceforth, and you shall be my servant.'

The king's son, seeing that he had foolishly placed himself in the power of the servant, promised readily everything his servant asked, and begged only to be drawn up.

But the faithless servant, without noticing his master's prayers, said roughly, 'You must make a solemn oath that you will not speak a word to any one about the change we are going to make.'

Of course, since the prince could not help himself, he took the oath at once, and then the servant drew him up, and they changed clothes. Then the wicked servant dressed himself in his master's fine clothes, mounted his master's horse, and rode forward on the journey, whilst the unfortunate prince, disguised in his servant's dress, walked beside him.

In this way they went on until they came to the court of the king to which the exiled son had been recommended by his father.

Faithful to his promise, the unfortunate price saw his false servant received at the court with great honours as the son of a great king, whilst he himself, all unnoticed, stood in the waiting-room with the servants, and was treated by them with all familiarity as their equal.

After having some time enjoyed to his heart's content the hospitalities the king lavished upon him, the false servant began to be afraid that his master's patience might be wearied out soon, under all the indignities to which he was exposed, and that one day he might be tempted to forget his oath and proclaim himself in his true character. Filled with these misgivings, the wicked man thought over all possible ways by which he could do away with his betrayed master without any danger to himself.

One day he thought he had found out a way to do this, and took the first opportunity to carry out his cruel plan.

Now you must know that the king at whose court this unhappy prince and the false servant were staying, kept in his gardens a great number of wild beasts fastened up in large cages. One morning, as the pretended prince was walking in these gardens with the king, he said suddenly, 'Your Majesty has a large number of very fine wild beasts, and I admire them very much; I think, however, it is a pity that you keep them always fastened up, and spend so much money over their food. Why not send them under a keeper to find their own food in the forest? I dare say your Majesty would be very glad if I recommended a man to you who could take them out in the morning and bring them back safely at night?'

The king asked, 'Do you really think, prince, that you can find me such a man?'

'Of course, I can,' replied unhesitatingly the cruel man; 'such a man is now in your Majesty's court. I mean my own servant. Only call him and threaten that you will have his head cut off if he does not do it, and compel him to accept the task. I dare say he will try to excuse himself, and say the thing is impossible, but only threaten him with the loss of his head whether he refuses or fails. For my part, I am quite willing your Majesty should have him put to death, if he disobeys.'

When the king heard this, he summoned the disguised prince before him, and said, 'I hear that you can do wonders: that you are able to drive wild beasts out like cattle to find their own food in the forest, and bring them back safely at night into their cages. Therefore, I order you this morning to drive all my bears into the forest, and to bring them back again in the evening. If you don't do this, your head will pay for it; so beware!'

The unlucky prince answered, 'I am not able to do this thing, so your Majesty had better cut off my head at once.'

But the king would not listen to him, only saying, 'We will wait until evening; *then* I shall surely have your head cut off unless you bring back all my bears safely to their cages.'

Now nothing was left for the poor prince to do but open the cage-doors and try his luck in driving the bears to the forest. The moment he opened the doors all the bears rushed out wildly, and disappeared quickly among the trees.

The prince followed them sadly into the forest, and sat down on a fallen tree to think over his hard fortunes. As he sat thus, he began to weep bitterly, for he saw no better prospect before him than to lose his head at night.

As he sat thus crying, a creature in form like a man, but covered all over with thick hair, came out of a neighbouring thicket, and asked him what he was crying for. Then the prince told him all that had happened to him, and that as all the bears had run away he expected to be beheaded at night when he returned without them. Hearing this, the wild man gave him a little bell, and said kindly, 'Don't be afraid! Only take care of this bell, and when you wish the bears to return, just ring it gently, and they will all come back and follow you quietly into their cages.' And having said this he went away.

When the sun began to go down, the prince rang the little bell gently, and, to his great joy, all the bears came dancing awkwardly round him, and let him lead them back to the gardens, following him like a flock of sheep, whilst he, pleased with his success, took out a flute and played little airs as he walked before them. In this way he was able to fasten them up again in their dens without the least trouble.

Every one at the court was astonished at this, and the false servant more than all the others, though he concealed his surprise, and said to the king, 'Your Majesty sees now that I told you the truth. I am quite sure the man can manage the wolves just as well as the bears, if you only threaten him as before.'

Thereupon, the next morning the king called the poor prince, and ordered him to lead out the wolves to find their food in the forest and to bring them back to their cages at night. 'Unless you do this,' said his Majesty, as before, 'you will lose your head.'

The prince pleaded vainly the impossibility of his doing such a thing; but the king would not hear him, only saying, 'You may as well try, for whether you refuse or fail you will certainly lose your head.'

So the prince was obliged to open the cages of the wolves, and the moment he did this the wild animals sprang past him into the thickets just as the bears had done, and he, following them slowly, went and sat down to bewail his ill-luck.

Whilst he sat thus weeping, the wild man came out of the wood and asked him, just as he had done the day before, what he was crying for. The prince told him, whereupon the creature gave him another little bell, and said, 'When you want the wolves to come back, just ring this bell, and they will all come and follow you.' Having said this he went back into the wood, and left the prince alone.

Just before it grew dark, the prince rang his bell, and to his great joy all the wolves came rushing up to him from all quarters of the forest, and followed him quietly back to their cages.

Seeing this, the false servant advised the king to send out the birds also, and to threaten the disguised prince with the loss of his head if he failed to bring them also back in the evening.

Accordingly the next morning the king ordered the prince to let out all the wild doves, and to bring them all safely to their different cages before night set in.

The instant the poor young man opened the cage-doors the wild doves rose like a cloud into the air, and vanished over the tops of the trees. So the prince went into the forest and sat down again on the fallen tree. As he sat there, thinking how hopeless a task he had now before him, he could not help crying aloud and bewailing all his past misfortunes and present miserable fate.

Hardly had he begun to lament, however, before the same wild man came from the bushes near him and asked what fresh trouble had befallen him. Then the prince told him. Thereupon the wild man gave him a third bell, saying, 'When you wish the wild doves to return to their cages you have only to ring this little bell.' And so it indeed happened, for the moment the prince began ringing softly, all the doves came flying about him, and he walked back to the palace gardens and shut them up in their different cages without the least trouble.

Now, happily for the prince, the king had just at this time much more important business on his hands than finding his wild beasts and birds in food without paying for it. No less a matter, in fact, began to occupy him than the finding a suitable husband for his daughter. For this purpose he sent out a proclamation that he would hold races during three days, and would reward the victor of each day with a golden apple. Whosoever should succeed in winning all three apples should have the young princess for his wife. Now this princess was far more beautiful than any other princess in the world, and an exceeding great number of knights prepared to try and win her. This, the poor prince in his servant's dress watched with great dismay; for he had fallen deeply in love with the fair daughter of the king. So he puzzled himself day and night with plans how he, too, could try his luck in the great race.

At last he determined to go into the forest and ask the wild man to help him. When the wild man heard the prince calling, he came out of the thicket, and listened to all he had to say about the matter. Seeing how much the prince was interested in the young princess, who was to be the prize of the victor, the wild man brought out some handsome clothes and a fine horse, and gave them to the prince, saying, 'When you start in a race, do not urge your horse too much, but at the end, when you are getting near the goal, spur him, and then you will be sure to win. Don't forget, however, to bring me the golden apple as soon as you receive it.'

All came to pass just as the wild man had said. The prince won the apples the two first days; but as he disappeared as soon as he received them from the king, no one in the court recognised him in his fine attire, and all wondered greatly who the stranger knight might be. As for the king, he was more perplexed and curious than all the rest, and determined not to let the stranger escape so easily the third day. So he ordered a deep, wide ditch to be dug at the end of the race-course, and a high wall built beyond it, thinking thus to stop the victor and find out who he was.

The prince, hearing of the king's orders, and guessing the reason of them, went once again into the forest to ask help from his wild friend. The wild man, thereupon, brought out to him a still more beautiful racer, and a suit of splendid clothes; and, thus prepared, the prince took his place as before among the knights who were going to try for the prize. He won the golden apple this third time also; but, to the surprise of the king and the whole court, who hoped now to find out who he was, he made his horse spring lightly over the ditch, and the great wall, and vanished again in the forest.

The king tried every way to find out who had won the three golden apples, but all in vain. At last, one day, the princess, walking in the gardens of the palace, met the prince disguised in his servant's dress, and saw the shining of the three apples which he carried concealed in his bosom. Thereupon she ran at once to her father, and told him what she had seen, and the king, wondering very much, called the servant before him.

Now the prince thought it time to put an end to all his troubles, and therefore told the king frankly all his misfortunes. He related how he had offended the king, his father, and been exiled for life; how his false servant had betrayed him; and how the wild man he had set free had come to help him out of the fearful snares the wicked servant had spread for him.

After hearing all this, the king very gladly gave him the princess for wife, and ordered the false servant to be put to death immediately.

As for the prince, he lived with his beautiful princess very happily for many years after this, and when the king, his father-in-law, died, he left to them both the kingdom.

THE BITER BIT.

ONCE upon a time there was an old man who, whenever he heard anyone complain how many sons he had to care for, always laughed and said, 'I wish that it would please God to give me a hundred sons!'

This he said in jest; as time, however, went on he had, in reality, neither more nor less than a hundred sons.

He had trouble enough to find different trades for his sons, but when they were once all started in life they worked diligently and gained plenty of money. Now, however, came a fresh difficulty. One day the eldest son came in to his father and said, 'My dear father, I think it is quite time that I should marry.'

Hardly had he said these words before the second son came in, saying, 'Dear father, I think it is already time that you were looking out for a wife for me.'

A moment later came in the third son, asking, 'Dear father, don't you think it is high time that you should find me a wife?' In like manner came the fourth and fifth, until the whole hundred had made a similar request. All of them wished to marry, and desired their father to find wives for them as soon as he could.

The old man was not a little troubled at these requests; he said, however, to his sons, 'Very well, my sons, I have nothing to say against your marrying; there is, however, I foresee, one great difficulty in the way. There are one hundred of you asking for wives, and I hardly think we can find one hundred marriageable girls in all the fifteen villages which are in our neighbourhood'

To this the sons, however, answered, 'Don't be anxious about that, but mount your horse and take in your sack sufficient engagement-cakes. You must take, also, a stick in your hand so that you can cut a notch in it for every girl you see. It does not signify whether she be handsome or ugly, or lame or blind, just cut a notch in your stick for every one you meet with.'

The old man said, 'Very wisely spoken, my sons! I will do exactly as you tell me.'

Accordingly he mounted his horse, took a sack full of cakes on his shoulder and a long stick in his hand, and started off at once to beat up the neighbourhood for girls to marry his sons.

The old man had travelled from village to village during a whole month, and whenever he had seen a girl he cut a notch in his stick. But he was getting pretty well tired, and he began to count how many notches he had already made. When he had counted them carefully over and over again, to be certain that he had counted all, he could only make out seventy-four, so that still twenty-six were wanting to complete the number required. He was, however, so weary with his month's ride, that he determined to return home. As he rode along, he saw a priest driving oxen yoked to a plough, and seemingly very deep in anxious thought about something. Now the old man wondered a little to see the priest ploughing his own corn-fields without even a boy to help him, he therefore shouted to ask him why he drove his oxen himself. The priest, however, did not even turn his head to see who called to him, so intent was he in urging on his oxen and in guiding his plough.

The old man thought he had not spoken loud enough, so he shouted out again as loud as he could, 'Stop your oxen a little, and tell me why you are ploughing yourself without even a lad to help you, and this, too, on a holyday?'

Now the priest—who was in a perspiration with his hard work—answered testily, 'I conjure you by your old age, leave me in peace! I cannot tell you my ill-luck.'

At this answer, however, the old man was only the more curious, and persisted all the more earnestly in asking questions to find out why the priest ploughed on a Saint's day. At last the priest, tired with his importunity, sighed deeply and said, 'Well, if you *will* know: I am the only man in my household, and God has blessed me with a hundred daughters!'

The old man was overjoyed at hearing this, and exclaimed cheerfully, 'That's very good! It is just what I want, for *I* have a hundred sons, and so, as you have a hundred daughters, we can be friends!'

The moment the priest heard this he became pleasant and talkative, and invited the old man to pass the night in his house. Then, leaving his plough in the field, he drove the oxen back to the village. Just before reaching his house, however, he said to the old man, 'Go yourself into the house whilst I tie up my oxen.'

No sooner, however, had the old man entered the yard than the wife of the priest rushed at him with a big stick, crying out, 'We have not bread enough for our hundred daughters, and we want neither beggars nor visitors,' and with these words she drove him away.

Shortly afterwards the priest came out of the barn, and, finding the old man sitting on the road before the gate, asked him why he had not gone into the house as he had told him to do. Whereupon the old man replied, 'I went in, but your wife drove me away!'

Then the priest said, 'Only wait here a moment till I come back to fetch you.' He then went quickly into his house and scolded his wife right well, saying, 'What have you done? What a fine chance you have spoiled! The man who came in was going to be our friend, for he has a hundred sons who would gladly have married our hundred daughters!'

When the wife heard this she changed her dress hastily, and arranged her hair and head-dress in a different fashion. Then she smiled very sweetly, and welcomed with the greatest possible politeness the old man, when her husband led him into the house. In fact, she pretended that she knew nothing at all of any one having been driven away from their door. And as the old man wanted much to find wives for his sons, he also pretended that he did not know that the smiling housemistress and the woman who drove him away with a stick were one and the self-same person.

So the old man passed the night in the house, and next morning asked the priest formally to give him his hundred daughters for wives for his hundred sons. Thereupon the priest answered that he was quite willing, and had already spoken to his daughters about the matter, and that they, too, were all quite willing. Then the old man took out his 'engagement-cakes,' and put them on the table beside him, and gave each of the girls a piece of money to *mark* them. Then each of the engaged girls sent a small present by him to that one of his sons to whom she was thus betrothed. These gifts the old man put in the bag wherein he had carried the 'engagement-cakes.' He then mounted his horse, and rode off merrily homewards.

There were great rejoicings in his household when he told how successful he had been in his search, and that he really had found a hundred girls ready and willing to be married; and these hundred, too, a priest's daughters.

The sons insisted that they should begin to make the wedding preparations without delay and commenced at once to invite the guests who were to form part of the wedding procession to go to the priest's house and bring home the brides.

Here, however, another difficulty occurred. The old father must find two hundred *brideleaders* (two for each bride) one hundred *kooms* (first witnesses); one hundred *starisvats* (second witnesses); one hundred *chaious* (running footmen who go before the processions) and three hundred *vojvodes* (standard-bearers); and, besides these, a respectable number of other non-official guests.*

To find all these persons the father had to hunt throughout the neighbourhood for three years; at last, however, they were all found, and a day was appointed when they were to meet at his house and go thence in procession to the house of the priest.

On the appointed day all the invited guests gathered at the old man's house. With great noise and confusion, after a fair amount of feasting, the wedding procession was formed properly, and set out for the house of the priest where the hundred brides were already prepared for their departure for their new home.

So great was the confusion, indeed, that the old man quite forgot to take with him one of the hundred sons, and never missed him in the greeting and talking and drinking he was obliged, as father of the bridegrooms, to go through. Now the young man had worked so long and so hard in preparing for the wedding-day that he never woke up till long after the procession had started and every one had had, like his father, too much to do and too many things to think of to miss him.

The wedding procession arrived in good order at the

* See 'Popular Customs of Serbia,' by the same author.

priest's house, where a feast was already spread out for them. Having done honour to the various good things, and having gone through all the ceremonies usual on such occasions, the hundred brides were given over to their 'leaders,' and the procession started on its return to the old man's house. But, as they did not set off until pretty late in the afternoon, it was decided that the night should be spent somewhere on the road. When they came, therefore, to a certain river named 'Luckless,' as it was already dark, some of the men proposed that the party should pass the night by the side of the water without crossing over. However, some others of the chief of the party so warmly advised the crossing the river and encamping on the other bank, that this course was at length, after a very lively discussion, determined on; accordingly the procession began to move over the bridge.

Just, however, as the wedding party were half-way across the bridge its two sides began to draw nearer each other, and pressed the people so close together that they had hardly room to breathe—much less could they move forwards or backwards.

They were kept for some time in this position, some shouting and scolding, others quiet because frightened, until at length a black giant appeared, and shouted to them in a terribly loud voice, 'Who are you all? Where do you come from? Where are you going?'

Some of the bolder among them answered, 'We are going to our old friend's house, taking home the hundred brides for his hundred sons; but unluckily we ventured on this bridge after nightfall, and it has pressed us so tightly together that we cannot move one way or the other.'

'And where is your old friend?' inquired the black giant.

Now all the wedding guests turned their eyes towards the old man. Thereupon he turned towards the giant, who instantly said to him, 'Listen, old man! Will you give me what you have forgotten at home, if I let your friends pass over the bridge?'

The old man considered some time what it might be that he had forgotten at home, but, at last, not being able to recollect anything in particular that he had left, and hearing on all sides the groans and moans of his guests, he replied, 'Well, I will give it you, if you will only let the procession pass over.'

Then the black giant said to the party, 'You all hear what he has promised, and are all my witnesses to the bargain. In three days I shall come to fetch what I have bargained for.'

Having said this, the black giant widened the bridge and the whole procession passed on to the other bank in safety. The people, however, no longer wished to spend the night on the way, so they moved on as fast as they could, and early in the morning reached the old man's house.

As everybody talked of the strange adventure they had met with, the eldest son, who had been left at home, soon began to understand how the matter stood, and went to his father saying, 'O my father! you have sold *me* to the black giant!'

Then the old man was very sorry, and troubled; but his friends comforted him, saying, 'Don't be frightened! nothing will come of it.'

The marriage ceremonies were celebrated with great rejoicings. Just, however, as the festivities were at their height, on the third day, the black giant appeared at the gate and shouted, 'Now, give me at once what you have promised.'

The old man, trembling all over, went forward and asked him, 'What do you want?'

'Nothing but what you have promised me!' returned the black giant.

As he could not break his promise, the old man, very much distressed, was then obliged to deliver up his eldest son to the giant, who thereupon said, 'Now I shall take your son with me, but after three years have passed you can come to the Luckless River and take him away.'

Having said this the black giant disappeared, taking with him the young man, whom he carried off to his workshop as an apprentice to the trade of witchcraft.

From that time the poor old man had not a single moment of happiness. He was always sad and anxious, and counted every year, and month, and week, and even every day, until the dawn of the last day of the three years. Then he took a staff in his hand and hurried off to the bank of the river Luckless. As soon as he reached the river, he was met by the black giant, who asked him, 'Why are you come?' The old man answered that he had come to take home his son, according to his agreement.

Thereupon the giant brought out a tray on which stood a sparrow, a turtle-dove, and a quail, and said to the old man, 'Now, if you can tell which of these is your son, you may take him away.'

The poor old father looked intently at the three birds, one after the other, and over and over again, but at last he was forced to own that he could not tell which of them was his son. So he was obliged to go away by himself, and was far more miserable than before. He had hardly, however, got half-way home when he thought he would go back to the river and take one of the birds which he remembered had looked at him intently.

When he reached the river Luckless he was again met by the black giant, who brought out the tray again, and placed on it this time a partridge, a tit-mouse, and a thrush, saying, 'Now, my old man, find out which is your son!'

The anxious father again looked at one bird after the other, but he felt more uncertain than before, and so, crying bitterly, again went away.

Just as the old man was going through a forest, which was between the river Luckless and his house, an old woman met him, and said, 'Stop a moment! Where are you hurrying to? And why are you in such trouble?' Now, the old man was so deeply musing over his great unhappiness that he did not at first attend to the old woman; but she followed him, calling after him, and repeating her questions with more earnestness. So he stopped at last, and told her what a terrible misfortune had fallen upon him. When the old woman had listened to the whole story, she said cheerfully, 'Don't be cast down! Don't be afraid! Go back again to the river, and, when the giant brings out the three birds, look into their eyes sharply. When you see that one of the birds has a tear in one of its eyes, seize that bird and hold it fast, for it has a human soul.'

The old man thanked her heartily for her advice, and turned back, for the third time, towards the Luckless River. Again the black giant appeared, and looked very merry whilst he brought out his tray and put upon it a sparrow, a dove, and a woodpecker, saying, 'My old man! find out which is your son!' Then the father looked sharply into the eyes of the birds, and saw that from the right eye of the dove a tear dropped slowly down. In a moment he grasped the bird tightly, saying, 'This is my son!' The next moment he found himself holding fast his eldest son by the shoulder, and so, singing and shouting in his great joy, took him quickly home, and gave him over to his eldest daughter-in-law, the wife of his son.

Now, for some time they all lived together very happily. One day, however, the young man said to his father, 'Whilst I was apprentice in the workshop of the black giant, I learned a great many tricks of witchcraft. Now I intend to change myself into a fine horse, and you shall take me to market and sell me for a good sum of money. But be sure not to give up the halter.'

The father did as the son had said. Next market day he went to the city with a fine horse which he offered for sale. Many buyers came round him, admiring the horse, and bidding large sums for it, so that at last the old man was able to sell it for two thousand ducats. When he received the money, he took good care not to let go the halter, and he returned home far richer than he ever dreamt of being.

A few days later, the man who had bought the horse sent his servant with it to the river to bathe, and, whilst in the water, the horse got loose from the servant and galloped off into the neighbouring forest. There he changed himself back into his real shape, and returned to his father's house.

After some time had passed, the young man said one day to his father, 'Now I will change myself into an ox, and you can take me to market to sell me; but take care not to give up the rope with which you lead me.'

So next market-day the old man went to the city leading a very fine ox, and soon found a buyer, who offered him ten times the usual price paid for an ox. The buyer asked also for the rope to lead the animal home, but the old man said, 'What do you want with such an old thing? You had better buy a new one!' and he went off taking with him the rope.

That evening, whilst the servants of the buyer were driving the ox to the field, he ran away into a wood near, and, having taken there his human shape, returned home to his father's house.

On the eve of the next market-day, the young man said to his father, 'Now I will change myself into a cow with golden horns, and you can sell me as before, only take care not to give up the string.'

Accordingly he changed himself next morning into a cow, and the old man took it to the market-place, and asked for it three hundred crowns.

But the black giant had learnt that his former apprentice was making a great deal of money by practising the trade he had taught him, and, being jealous at this, he determined to put an end to the young man's gains.

Therefore, on the third day he came to the market himself as a buyer, and the moment he saw the beautiful cow with golden horns he knew that it could be no other than his former apprentice. So he came up to the old man, and, having outbid all the other would-be purchasers, paid at once the price he had agreed on. Having done this, he caught the string in his hand, and tried to wrench it from the terrified old man, who called out, 'I have not sold you the string, but the cow!' and held the string as fast as he could with both hands.

'Oh, no!' said the buyer, 'I have the law and custom on my side! Whoever buys a cow, buys also the string with which it is led!' Some of the amused and astonished lookers-on said that this was quite true, therefore the old man was obliged to give up the string.

The black giant, well satisfied with his purchase, took the cow with him to his castle, and, after having put

o

iron chains on her legs, fastened her in a cellar. Every morning the giant gave the cow some water and hay, but he never unchained her.

One evening, however, the cow, with incessant struggles, managed to get free from the chains, and immediately opened the cellar-door with her horns and ran away.

Next morning the black giant went as usual into the cellar, carrying the hay and water for the cow; but seeing she had got free and run away, he threw the hay down, and started off at once to pursue her.

When he came within sight of her, he turned himself into a wolf and ran at her with great fury; but his clever apprentice changed himself instantly from a cow into a bear, whereupon the giant turned himself from a wolf into a lion; the bear then turned into a tiger, and the lion changed into a crocodile, whereupon the tiger turned into a sparrow. Upon this the giant changed from the form of a crocodile into a hawk, and the apprentice immediately changed into a hare; on seeing which, the hawk became a greyhound. Then the apprentice changed from a hare into a falcon, and the greyhound into an eagle; whereupon the apprentice changed into a fish. The giant then turned from an eagle into a mouse, and immediately the apprentice, as a cat, ran after him; then the giant turned himself into a heap of millet, and the apprentice transformed himself into a hen and chickens, which very greedily picked up all the millet except one single seed, in which the master was, who changed himself into a squirrel;

instantly, however, the apprentice became a hawk, and, pouncing on the squirrel, killed it.

In this way the apprentice beat his master, the black giant, and revenged himself for all the sufferings he had endured whilst learning the trade of witchcraft. Having killed the squirrel, the hawk took his proper shape again, and the young man returned joyfully to his father, whom he made immensely rich.

THE TRADE THAT NO ONE KNOWS.

A LONG while ago there lived a poor old couple, who had an only son. The old man and his wife worked very hard to nourish their child well and bring him up properly, hoping that he, in return, would take care of them in their old age.

When, however, the boy had grown up, he said to his parents, 'I am a man now, and I intend to marry, so I wish you to go at once to the king and ask him to give me his daughter for wife.' The astonished parents rebuked him, saying, 'What can you be thinking of? We have only this poor hut to shelter us, and hardly bread enough to eat, and we dare not presume to go into the king's presence, much less can we venture to ask for his daughter to be your wife.'

The son, however, insisted that they should do as he said, threatening that if they did not comply with his wishes he would leave them, and go away into the world. Seeing that he was really in earnest in what he said, the unhappy parents promised him they would go and ask for the king's daughter. Then the old mother made a wedding cake in her son's presence, and, when it was ready, she put it in a bag, took her staff in her hand, and went straight to the palace where the king lived. There the king's servants bade her come in, and led her into the hall where his Majesty was accustomed to receive the poor people who came to ask alms or to present petitions.

The poor old woman stood in the hall, confused and ashamed at her worn-out, shabby clothes, and looking as if she were made of stone, until the king said to her kindly, 'What do *you* want from me, old mother?'

She dared not, however, tell his Majesty why she had come, so she stammered out in her confusion, 'Nothing, your Majesty.'

Then the king smiled a little and said, 'Perhaps you come to ask alms?'

Then the old woman, much abashed, replied, 'Yes, your Majesty, if you please!'

Thereupon the king called his servants and ordered them to give the old woman ten crowns, which they did. Having received this money, she thanked his Majesty, and returned home, saying to herself, 'I dare say when my son sees all this money he will not think any more of going away from us.'

In this thought, however, she was quite mistaken, for no sooner had she entered the hut than the son came to her and asked impatiently, 'Well, mother, have you done as I asked you?'

At this she exclaimed, 'Do give up, once for all, this silly fancy, my son. How could you expect me to ask the king for his daughter to be your wife? That would be a bold thing for a rich nobleman to do, how then can *we* think of such a thing? Anyhow, *I* dared not say one word to the king about it. But only look what a lot of money I have brought back. Now you can look for a wife suitable for you, and then you will forget the king's daughter.'

When the young man heard his mother speak thus, he grew very angry, and said to her, 'What do I want with the king's money? I don't want his money, but I *do* want his daughter! I see you are only playing with me, so I shall leave you. I will go away somewhere—anywhere—wherever my eyes lead me.'

Then the poor old parents prayed and begged him not to go away from them, and leave them alone in their old age; but they could only quiet him by promising faithfully that the mother should go again next day to the king, and this time really ask him to give his daughter to her son for a wife.

In the morning, therefore, the old woman went again to the palace, and the servants showed her into the same hall she had been in before. The king, seeing her stand there, inquired, 'What want you, my old woman, now?'

She was, however, so ashamed that she could hardly stammer, 'Nothing, please your Majesty.'

The king, supposing that she came again to beg, ordered his servants to give her this time also ten crowns.

With this money the poor woman returned to her hut, where her son met her, asking, 'Well, mother, *this* time

I hope you have done what I asked you?' But she replied, 'Now, my dear son, do leave the king's daughter in peace. How can you really think of such a thing? Even if she would marry you, where is the house to bring her to? So be quiet, and take this money which I have brought you.'

At these words the son was more angry than before, and said sharply, 'As I see you will not let me marry the king's daughter, I will leave you this moment and never come back again;' and, rushing out of the hut, he ran away. His parents hurried after him, and at length prevailed on him to return, by swearing to him that his mother should go again to the king next morning, and really and in truth ask his Majesty this time for his daughter.

So the young man agreed to go back home and wait until the next day.

On the morrow the old woman, with a heavy heart, went to the palace, and was shown as before into the king's presence. Seeing her there for the third time, his Majesty asked her impatiently, 'What do you want this time, old woman?' And she, trembling all over, said, 'Please your Majesty—nothing.' Then the king exclaimed, 'But it cannot be nothing. Something you must want, so tell me the truth at once, if you value your life!' Thereupon the old woman was forced to tell all the story to the king; how her son had a great desire to marry the princess, and so had forced her to come and ask the king to give her to him for wife.

When the king had heard everything, he said, 'Well,

after all, *I* shall say nothing against it if my daughter will consent to it.' He then told his servants to lead the princess into his presence. When she came he told her all about the affair, and asked her, 'Are you willing to marry the son of this old woman?'

The princess answered, 'Why not? If only he learns first the trade that no one knows!' Thereupon the king bade his attendants give money to the poor woman, who now went back to her hut with a light heart.

The moment she entered, her son asked her, 'Have you engaged her?' And she returned, 'Do let me get my breath a little! Well, *now* I have really asked the king; but it is of no use, for the princess declares she will not marry you until you have learnt the trade that no one knows!'

'Oh, that matters nothing!' exclaimed the son. 'Now I only know the condition, it's all right!' The next morning the young man set out on his travels through the world in search of a man who could teach him the trade that no one knows. He wandered about a long time without being able to find out where he could learn such a trade. At length one day, being quite tired out with walking and very sad, he sat down on a fallen log by the wayside. After he had sat thus a little while, an old woman came up to him, and asked, 'Why art thou so sad, my son?' And he answered, 'What is the use of your asking, when you cannot help me?' But she continued, 'Only tell me what is the matter, and perhaps I can help you.' Then he said, 'Well, if you must know, the matter is this: I have been travelling about the world a long time to find a master who can teach me the trade which no one knows.' 'Oh, if it is only that,' cried the old woman, 'just listen to me! Don't be afraid, but go straight into the forest which lies before you, and there you will find what you want.'

The young man was very glad to hear this, and got up at once and went to the forest. When he had gone pretty far in the wood, he saw a large castle, and, whilst he stood looking at it and wondering what it was, four giants came out of it and ran up to him, shouting, 'Do you wish to learn the trade that no one knows?' He said, 'Yes; that is just the reason why I come here.' Whereupon they took him into the castle.

Next morning the giants prepared to go out hunting, and, before leaving, they said to him, 'You must on no account go into the first room by the dining-hall.' Hardly, however, were the giants well out of sight before the young man began to reason thus with himself: 'I see very well that I have come into a place from which I shall never go out alive with my head, so I may as well see what is in the room, come what may afterwards.' So he went and opened the door a little and peeped in. There stood a golden ass, bound to a golden manger. He looked at it a little, and was just going to shut the door when the ass said, 'Come and take the halter from my head, and keep it hidden about you. It will serve you well if you only understand how to use it.' So he took the halter, and, after fastening the room door, quickly concealed it under his clothes. He had not sat very long before the giants came home. They asked him at once if he had been in the first room, and he, much frightened, replied, 'No, I have not been in.' 'But we know that you have been!' said the giants in great anger, and seizing some large sticks, they beat him so severely that he could hardly stand on his feet. It was very lucky for him that he had the halter wound round his body under his clothes, or else he would certainly have been killed.

The next day the giants again prepared to go out hunting, but before leaving him they ordered him on no account to enter the second room.

Almost as soon as the giants had gone away he became so very curious to see what might be in the second room, that he could not resist going to the door. He stood there a little, thinking within himself, 'Well, I am already more dead than alive, much worse cannot happen to me!' and so he opened the door and looked in. There he was surprised to see a very beautiful girl, dressed all in gold and silver, who sat combing her hair, and setting in every tress a large diamond. He stood admiring her a little while, and was just going to shut the door again, when she spoke, 'Wait a minute, young man. Come and take this key, and mind you keep it safely. It will serve you some time, if you only know how to use it.' So he went in and took the key from the girl, and then, going out, fastened the door and went and sat down in the same place he had sat before.

He had not remained there very long before the giants came home from hunting. The moment they entered the house they took up their large sticks to beat him, asking, at the same time, whether he had been in the second room.

Shaking all over with fear, he answered them, 'No, I have not!'

'But we know that you have been,' shouted the giants in great anger, and they then beat him worse than on the first day.

The next morning, as the giants went out as usual to hunt, they said to him, 'Do not go into the third room, for anything in the world; for if you do go in we shall not forgive you as we did yesterday, and the day before! We shall kill you outright!' No sooner, however, had the giants gone out of sight, than the young man began to say to himself, 'Most likely they will kill me, whether I go into the room or not. Besides, if they do not kill me, they have beaten me so badly already that I am sure I cannot live long, so, anyhow, I will go and see what is in the third room.' Then he got up and went and opened the door.

He was quite shocked, however, when he saw that the room was full of human heads! These heads belonged to young men who had come, like himself, to learn the trade that no one knows, and who, having obeyed faithfully and strictly the orders of the giants, had been killed by them.

The young man was turning quickly to go away, when one of the heads called out, 'Don't be afraid, but come in!' Thereupon he went into the room. Then the head gave him an iron chain, and said, 'Take care of this chain, for it will serve you some time if you know how to use it!' So he took the chain, and going out fastened the door.

He went and sat down in the usual place to wait for the coming home of the giants, and, as he waited, he grew quite frightened, for he fully expected that they would really kill him this time.

The instant the giants came home they took up their thick sticks and began to beat him without stopping to ask anything. They beat him so terribly that he was all but dead; then they threw him out of the house, saying to him, 'Go away now, since you have learnt the trade that no one knows!' When he had lain a long time on the ground where they had thrown him, feeling very sore and miserable, at length he tried to move away, saying to himself, 'Well, if they really have taught me the trade that no one knows, for the sake of the king's daughter I can suffer gladly all this pain, if I can only win her!'

After travelling for a long time, the young man came at last to the palace of the king whose daughter he wished to marry. When he saw the palace, he was exceedingly sad, and remembered the words of the princess; for, after all his wanderings and sufferings, he had learnt no trade, and had never been able to find what trade it was 'that no one knows.' Whilst considering what he had better do, he suddenly recollected the halter, the key, and the iron chain, which he had carried concealed about him ever since he left the castle of the four giants. He then said to himself, 'Let me see what these things can do!' So he took the halter and struck the earth with it, and immediately a handsome horse, beautifully caparisoned, stood before him. Then he struck the ground with the iron chain, and instantly a hare and a greyhound appeared, and the hare began to run quickly and the greyhound to follow her. In a moment the young man hardly knew himself, for he found himself in a fine hunting-dress, riding on the horse after the hare, which took a path that passed immediately under the windows of the king's palace. Now, it happened that the king stood at a window looking out, and noticed at once the beautiful greyhound which was chasing the hare, and the very handsome horse which a huntsman in a splendid dress was mounted on. The king was so pleased with the appearance of the horse and the greyhound, that he called instantly some of his servants, and, sending them after the strange rider, bade them invite him to come to the palace. The young man, however, hearing some people coming behind him calling and shouting, rode quickly behind a thick bush, and shook a little the halter and the iron chain. In a moment the horse, the greyhound, and the hare had vanished, and he found himself sitting on the ground under the trees dressed in his old shabby clothes. By this time the king's servants had come up, and, seeing him sit there, they asked him whether he had seen a fine huntsman on a beautiful horse pass that way. But he answered them rudely, 'No! I have not seen anyone pass, neither do I care to look to see who passes!'

Then the king's servants went on and searched the forest, calling and shouting as loudly as they could, but it was all in vain; they could neither see nor hear anything of the hunter. At length they went back to the king, and told him that the horse the huntsman rode was so exceedingly quick that they could not hear anything of him in the forest.

The young man now resolved to go to the hut where his old parents lived; and they were glad to see that he had come back to them once more.

Next morning, the son said to his father, 'Now, father, I will show you what I have learned. I will change myself into a beautiful horse, and you must lead me into the city and sell me, but be very careful not to give away the halter, or else I shall remain always a horse!' Accordingly, in a moment he changed himself into a horse of extraordinary beauty, and the father took him to the market-place to sell him. Very soon a great number of people gathered round the horse, wondering at his unusual beauty, and very high prices were offered for him; the old man, however, raised the price higher and higher at every offer. The news spread quickly about the city that a wonderfully handsome horse was for sale in the market-place, and at length the king himself heard of it, and sent some servants to bring the horse, that he might see it. The old man led the horse at once before the palace, and the king, after looking at it for some time with great admiration, could not help exclaiming, 'By my word, though I am a king, I never yet saw, much less rode, so handsome a horse!' Then he asked the old man if he would sell it him. 'I will sell it to your Majesty, very willingly,' said the old man; 'but I will sell only the horse, and not the halter.' Thereupon the king laughed, saying, 'What should I want with your dirty halter? For such a horse I will have a halter of gold made!' So the horse was sold to the king for a very high price, and the old man returned home with the money.

Next morning, however, there was a great stir and much consternation in the royal stables, for the beautiful horse had vanished somehow during the night. And at the time when the horse disappeared, the young man returned to his parents' hut.

A day or two afterwards the young man said to his father, 'Now I will turn myself into a fine church not far from the king's palace, and if the king wishes to buy it you may sell it him, only be sure not to part with the key or else I must remain always a church!'

When the king got up that morning, and went to his window to look out, he saw a beautiful church which he had never noticed before. Then he sent his servants out to see what it was, and soon after they came back saying, that 'the church belonged to an old pilgrim, who told them that he was willing to sell it if the king wished to buy it.' Then the king sent to ask what price he would sell it for, and the pilgrim replied, 'It is worth a great deal of money.'

Whilst the servants were bargaining with the father an old woman came up. Now this was the same old woman who had sent the young man to the castle of the four giants, and she herself had been there and had learnt the trade that no one knew. As she understood at once all about the church, and had no mind to have a rival in the trade, she resolved to put an end to the young man. For this purpose she began to outbid the king, and offered, at last, so very large a sum of ready money, that the old man was quite astonished and confused at seeing the money which she showed him. He accordingly accepted her offer, but whilst he was counting the money, quite forgot about the key. Before long, however, he recollected what his son had said, and then, fearing some mischief, he ran after the old woman and demanded the key back. But the old woman could not be persuaded to give back the key, and said it belonged to the church which she had bought and paid for. Seeing she would not give up the key, the old man grew more and more alarmed, lest some ill should befall his son, so he took hold of the old woman by the neck and forced her to drop the key. She struggled very hard to get it back again, and, whilst the old man and she wrestled together, the key changed itself suddenly into a dove and flew away high in the air over the palace gardens.

When the old woman saw this, she changed herself into a hawk and chased the dove. Just, however, as the hawk was about to pounce upon it, the dove turned itself into a beautiful bouquet, and dropped down into the hand of the king's daughter who happened to be walking in the garden. Then the hawk changed again into the old woman, who went to the gate of the palace and begged very hard that the princess would give her that bouquet, or, at least, one single flower from it.

But the princess said, 'No! not for anything in the world! These flowers fell to me from heaven!' The old woman, however, was determined to get one flower from the bouquet, so, seeing the princess would not hear her, she went straight to the king, and begged piteously that he would order his daughter to give her one of the flowers from her bouquet. The king, thinking the old woman wanted one of the flowers to cure some disease, called his daughter to him, and told her to give one to the beggar.

But just as the king said this, the bouquet changed itself into a heap of millet-seed and scattered itself all over the ground. Then the old woman quickly changed herself into a hen and chickens, and began greedily to pick up the seeds. Suddenly, however, the millet vanished, and in its place appeared a fox, which sprang on the hen and killed her.

Then the fox changed into the young man, who explained to the astonished king and princess that he it was who had demanded the hand of the princess, and that, in order to obtain it, he had wandered all over the world in search of some one who could teach him 'the trade that no one knows.'

When the king and his daughter heard this, they gladly fulfilled their part of the bargain, seeing how well the young man had fulfilled his.

Then, shortly afterwards, the king's daughter married the son of the poor old couple; and the king built for the princess and her husband a palace close to his own. There they lived long and had plenty of children, and people say that some of their descendants are living at present, and that these go constantly to pray in the church, which is always open because the key of it turned itself into a young man who married the king's daughter, after he had shown to her that he had done as she wished, and learnt, for her sake, 'the trade that no one knows.'

THE THREE SUITORS.

IN a very remote country there formerly lived a king who had only one child,—an exceedingly beautiful daughter. The princess had a great number of suitors, and amongst them were three young noblemen, whom the king loved much. As, however, the king liked the three nobles equally well, he could not decide to which of the three he should give his daughter as a wife. One day, therefore, he called the three young noblemen to him, and said, 'Go all of you and travel about the world. The one of you who brings home the most remarkable thing shall become my son-in-law!"

The three suitors started at once on their travels, each of them taking opposite ways, and going in search of remarkable things into distant and different countries.

A long time had not passed before one of the young nobles found a wonderful carpet which would carry rapidly through the air whoever sat upon it.

Another of them found a marvellous telescope, through which he could see everybody and everything in the world, and even the many-coloured sands at the bottom of the great deep sea.

The third found a wonder-working ointment, which could cure every disease in the world, and even bring dead people back to life again.

Now the three noble travellers were far distant from each other when they found these wonderful things. But when the young man who had found the telescope looked through it he saw one of his former friends and present rivals walking with a carpet on his shoulder, and so he set out to join him. As he could always see, by means of his marvellous telescope, where the other nobleman was, he had no great difficulty in finding him, and when the two had met, they sat side by side on the wonderful carpet, and it carried them through the air until they had joined the third traveller.

One day, when each of them had been telling of the remarkable things he had seen in his travels, one of them exclaimed suddenly, 'Now let us see what the beautiful princess is doing, and where she is.' Then the noble who had found the telescope looked through it and saw, to his great surprise and dismay, that the king's daughter was lying very sick, and at the point of death. He told this to his two friends and rivals, and they, too, were as thunderstruck at the bad news—until the one who had found the wonder-working ointment, remembering it suddenly, exclaimed, 'I am sure I could cure her, if I could only reach the palace soon enough!' On hearing this, the noble who had found the wonderful carpet, cried out, 'Let us sit down on my carpet, and it will quickly carry us to the king's palace!'

Thereupon the three nobles gently placed themselves

on the carpet, which rose instantly in the air, and carried them direct to the king's palace.

The king received them immediately; but said very sadly, 'I am sorry for you; for all your travels have been in vain. My daughter is just dying, so she can marry none of you!'

But the nobleman who possessed the wonder-working ointment said respectfully, 'Do not fear, sire, the princess will not die!' And on being permitted to enter the apartment where she lay sick, he placed the ointment so that she could smell it. In a few moments the princess revived, and when her waiting-women had rubbed a little of the ointment in her skin she recovered so quickly that in a few days she was better than she had been before she was taken ill.

The king was so glad to have his daughter given back to him, as he thought, from the grave, that he declared that she should marry no one but the young nobleman whose wonderful ointment had cured her.

But now a great dispute arose between the three young nobles; the one who possessed the ointment affirmed that had he not found it the princess would have died, and could not, therefore, have married any one; the noble who owned the telescope declared that had he not found the wonderful telescope they would never have known that the princess was dying, and so his friend would not have brought the ointment to cure her; whilst the third noble proved to them that had he not found the wonderful carpet, neither the finding of the ointment nor the telescope would have helped the princess, since they could not have travelled such a great distance in time to save her.

The king, overhearing this dispute, called the young noblemen to him, and said to them, 'My lords, from what you have said, I see that I cannot, with justice, give my daughter to any of you; therefore, I pray you to give up altogether the idea of marrying her, and that you continue friends as you always were before you became rivals.'

The three young nobles saw that the king had decided justly; so they all left their native country, and went into a far-off desert to live like hermits. And the king gave the princess to another of his great nobles.

Many, many years had passed away since the marriage of the princess, when her husband was sent by her father to a distant country with which the king was waging war. The nobleman took his wife, the princess, with him, as he was uncertain how long he might be forced to remain abroad. Now it happened that a violent storm arose just as the vessel, in which the princess and her husband were, was approaching a strange coast, and in the height of the great tempest the ship dashed on some rocks, and went to pieces instantly. All the people on board perished in the waves, excepting only the princess, who clung very fast to a boat, and was carried by the wind and the tide to the sea-shore. There she found what seemed to be an uninhabited country, and, finding a small cave in a rock, she lived in it alone three years, feeding on wild herbs and fruits. She searched every day to find some way out of the forest which surrounded her cave, but could find none. One day, however, when she had wandered farther than usual from the cave where she lived, she came suddenly on another cave, which had, to her great astonishment, a small door. She tried over and over again to open the door, thinking she would pass the night in the cave; but all her efforts were unavailing, it was shut so fast. At length, however, a deep voice from within the cave called out, 'Who is at the door?'

At this the princess was so surprised that she could not answer for some moments; when, however, she had recovered a little, she said, 'Open me the door!' Immediately the door was opened from within, and she saw, with sudden terror, an old man with a thick grey beard reaching below his waist, and long white hair flowing over his shoulders.

What frightened the princess the more was her finding a man living here in the same desert where she had lived herself three years without seeing a single soul.

The hermit and the princess looked at each long and earnestly without saying a word. At length, however, the old man said, 'Tell me, are you an angel or a daughter of this world?'

Then the princess answered, 'Old man, let me rest a moment, and then I will tell you all about myself, and what brought me here!' So the hermit brought out some wild pears, and when the princess had taken some of them, she began to tell him who she was, and how she came in that desert. She said, 'I am a king's daughter, and once, many years ago, three young nobles of my father's court asked the king for my hand in marriage. Now the king had such an equal affection for all these three young men that he was unwilling to give pain to any of them, so he sent them to travel into distant countries, and promised to decide between them when they returned.

'The three noblemen remained a long time away; and whilst they were still abroad somewhere, I fell dangerously ill. I was just at the point of death, when they all three returned suddenly; one of them bringing a wonderful ointment which cured me at once; the two others brought each equally remarkable things—a carpet that would carry whoever sat on it through the air, and a telescope with which one could see everybody and everything in the world, even to the sands at the bottom of the sea.'

The princess had gone on thus far with her story, when the hermit suddenly interrupted her, saying, 'All that happened afterwards I know as well as you can tell me. Look at me, my daughter! I am one of those noblemen who sought to win your hand, and here is the wonderful telescope.' And the hermit brought out the instrument from a recess in the side of his cave before he continued, 'My two friends and rivals came with me to this desert. We parted, however, immediately, and have never met since. I know not whether they are living or dead, but I will look for them.'

Then the hermit looked through his telescope, and saw that the other two noblemen were living in caves like his, in different parts of the same desert. Having found this out, he took the princess by the hand, and led her on until they found the other hermits. When all were re-united, the princess related her adventures since the ship, in which her husband was, had gone down, and she alone had been saved.

The three noble hermits were pleased to see her alive once again, but at once decided that they ought to send her back to the king, her father.

Then they made the princess a present of the wonderful telescope, and the wonder-working ointment, and placed her on the wonderful carpet, which carried her and her treasures quickly and safely to her father's palace. As for the three noblemen, they remained, still living like hermits, in the desert, only they visited each other now and then, so that the years seemed no longer so tedious to them. For they had many adventures to relate to each other.

The king was exceedingly glad to receive his only child back safely, and the princess lived with her father many years but neither the king nor his daughter could entirely forget the three noble friends who, for her sake, lived like hermits in a wild desert in a far-off land.

THE GOLDEN-HAIRED TWINS.

ONCE upon a time, a long, long while ago, there lived a young king who wished very much to marry, but could not decide where he had better look for a wife.

One evening as he was walking disguised through the streets of his capital, as it was his frequent custom to do, he stopped to listen near an open window where he heard three young girls chatting gaily together.

The girls were talking about a report which had been lately spread through the city, that the king intended soon to marry.

One of the girls exclaimed, 'If the king would marry me I would give him a son who should be the greatest hero in the world.'

The second girl said, 'And if I were to be his wife I would present him with two sons at once. Two twins with golden hair.'

And the third girl declared that were the king to marry *her* she would give him a daughter so beautiful that there should not be her equal in the whole wide world!

The young king listened to all this, and for some time thought over their words, and tried to make up his mind which of the three girls he should choose for his wife. At last he decided that he would marry the one who had said she would bring him twins with golden hair.

Having once settled this in his own mind, he ordered that all preparations for his marriage should be made forthwith, and shortly after, when all was ready, he married the second girl of the three.

Several months after his marriage, the young king, who was at war with one of the neighbouring princes, received tidings of the defeat of his army, and heard that his presence was immediately required in the camp. He accordingly left his capital and went to his army, leaving the young queen in his palace to the care of his stepmother.

Now the king's stepmother hated her daughter-in-law very much indeed, so when the young queen was near her confinement, the old queen told her that it was always customary in the royal family for the heirs to the throne to be born in a garret.

The young queen (who knew nothing about the customs in royal families except what she had learnt from hearing or seeing since her marriage to the king) believed implicitly what her mother-in-law told her, although she thought it a great pity to leave her splendid apartments and go up into a miserable attic.

Now when the golden-haired twins were born, the old queen contrived to steal them out of their cradle, and put in their place two ugly little dogs. She then caused the two beautiful golden-haired boys to be buried alive in an out-of-the-way spot in the palace gardens, and then sent word to the king that the young queen had given him two little dogs instead of the heirs he was hoping for. The wicked step-mother said in her letter to the king that she herself was not surprised at this, though she was very sorry for his disappointment. As to herself, she had a long time suspected the young queen of having too great a friendship for goblins and elves, and all kinds of evil spirits.

When the king received this letter, he fell into a frightful rage, because he had only married the young girl in order to have the golden-haired twins she had promised him as heirs to his throne.

So he sent word back to the old queen that his wife should be put at once into the dampest dungeon in the castle, an order which the wicked woman took good care to see carried out without delay. Accordingly the poor young queen was thrown into a miserably dark dungeon under the palace, and kept on bread and water.

Now there was only a very small hole in this prison—hardly large enough to let in light and air—yet the old queen managed to cause a great many people to pass by this hole, and whoever passed was ordered to spit at and abuse the unhappy young queen, calling out to her, 'Are you really the queen? Are you the girl who cheated the king in order to be a queen? Where are your golden-haired twins? You cheated the king and your friends, and now the witches have cheated you!'

But the young king, though terribly angry and mortified at his great disappointment, was, at the same time, too sad and troubled to be willing to return to his palace. So he remained away for fully nine years. When he at last consented to return, the first thing he noticed in the palace gardens were two fine young trees, exactly the same size and the same shape.

These trees had both golden leaves and golden blossoms, and had grown up of themselves from the very spot where the stepmother of the king had buried the two golden-haired boys she had stolen from their cradle.

The king admired these two trees exceedingly, and was never weary of looking at them. This, however, did not at all please the old queen, for she knew that the two young princes were buried just where the trees grew, and she always feared that by some means what she had done would come to the king's ears. She therefore pretended that she was very sick, and declared that she was sure she should die unless her stepson, the king, ordered the two golden-leaved trees to be cut down, and a bed made for her out of their wood.

As the king was not willing to be the cause of her death, he ordered that her wishes should be attended to, notwithstanding he was exceedingly sorry to lose his favourite trees.

A bed was soon made from the two trees, and the seemingly sick old queen was laid on it as she desired. She was quite delighted that the golden-leaved trees had disappeared from the garden; but when midnight came, she could not sleep a bit, for it seemed to her that she heard the boards of which her bed was made in conversation with each other!

At last it seemed to her, that one board said, quite plainly, 'How are you, my brother?' And the other board answered, 'Thank you, I am very well; how are you?' 'Oh, I am all right,' returned the first board; 'but I wonder how our poor mother is in her dark dungeon! Perhaps she is hungry and thirsty!'

The wicked old queen could not sleep a minute all night, after hearing this conversation between the boards of her new bed; so next morning she got up very early and went to see the king. She thanked him for attending to her wish, and said she already was much better, but she felt quite sure she would never recover thoroughly unless the boards of her new bed were cut up and thrown into a fire. The king was sorry to lose entirely even the boards made out of his two favourite trees, nevertheless he could not refuse to use the means pointed out for his step-mother's perfect recovery.

So the new bed was cut to pieces and thrown into the fire. But whilst the boards were blazing and crackling, two sparks from the fire flew into the court-yard, and in the next moment two beautiful lambs with golden fleeces and golden horns were seen gambolling about the yard.

The king admired them greatly, and made many inquiries who had sent them there, and to whom they belonged. He even sent the public crier many times through the city, calling on the owners of the golden-fleeced lambs to appear and claim them; but no one came, so at length he thought he might fairly take them as his own property.

The king took very great care of these two beautiful lambs, and every day directed that they should be well fed and attended to; this, however, did not at all please his stepmother. She could not endure even to look on the lambs with their golden fleeces and golden horns, for they always reminded her of the golden-haired twins. So, in a little while she pretended again to be dangerously sick, and declared she felt sure she should soon die unless the two lambs were killed and cooked for her.

The king was even fonder of his golden-fleeced lambs than he had been of the golden-leaved trees, but he could not long resist the tears and prayers of the old queen, especially as she seemed to be very ill. Accordingly, the lambs were killed, and a servant was ordered to carry their golden fleeces down to the river and to wash the blood well out of them. But whilst the servant held them under the water, they slipped, in some way or another, out of his fingers, and floated down the stream, which just at that place flowed very rapidly. Now it happened that a hunter was passing near the river a little lower down, and, as he chanced to look in the water, he saw something strange in it. So he stepped into the stream, and soon fished out a small box which he carried to his house, and there opened it. To his unspeakably great surprise, he found in the box two golden-haired boys. Now the hunter had no children of his own; he therefore adopted the twins he had fished out of the river, and brought them up just as if they had been his own sons. When the twins were grown up into handsome young men, one of them said to his foster-father, 'Make us two suits of beggar's clothes, and let us go and wander a little about the world!' The hunter, however, replied and said, 'No, I will have a fine suit made for each of you, such as is fitting for two such noble-looking young men.' But as the twins begged hard that he should not spend his money uselessly in buying fine clothes, telling him that they wished to travel about as beggars, the hunter—who always liked to do as his two handsome foster-sons wished—did as they desired, and ordered two suits of clothes, like those worn by beggars, to be prepared for them. The two sons then dressed themselves up as beggars, and as well as they could hid their beautiful golden locks, and then set out to see the world. They took with them a gusle* and a cymbal, and maintained themselves with their singing and playing.

They had wandered about in this way some time when one day they came to the king's palace. As the afternoon was already pretty far advanced, the young musicians begged to be allowed to pass the night in one of the outbuildings belonging to the court, as they were poor men, and quite strangers in the city. The old queen, however, who happened to be just then in the courtyard saw them, and hearing their request, said sharply that beggars could not be permitted to enter any part of the king's palace. The two travellers said they had hoped to pay for their night's lodging by their

* 'Gusle,' one-stringed instrument on which the Servian bards accompany their recitation of ballads.

songs and music, as one of them played and sung to the gusle, and the other to the cymbal.

The old queen, however, was not moved by this, but insisted on their going away at once. Happily for the two brothers the king himself came out into the courtyard just as his stepmother angrily ordered them to go away, and at once directed his servants to find a place for the musicians to sleep in, and ordered them to provide the brothers with a good supper. After they had supped, the king commanded them to be brought before him that he might judge of their skill as musicians, and that their singing might help him to pass the time more pleasantly.

Accordingly, after the two young men had taken the refreshment provided for them, the servants took them into the king's presence, and they began to sing this ballad:—

'The pretty bird, the swallow, built her nest with care, in the palace of the king. In the nest she reared up happily two of her little ones. A black, ugly-looking bird, however, came to the swallow's nest to mar her happiness, and to kill her two little ones. And the ugly black bird succeeded in destroying the happiness of the poor little swallow; the little ones, however, although yet weak and unfledged, were saved, and, when they were grown up and able to fly, they came to look at the palace where their mother, the pretty swallow, had built her nest.'

This strange song the two minstrels sung so very sweetly that the king was quite charmed, and asked them the meaning of the words.

Whereupon the two meanly dressed young men took off their hats, so that the rich tresses of their golden hair fell down over their shoulders, and the light glanced so brightly upon it that the whole hall was illuminated by the shining. They then stepped forward together, and told the king all that had happened to them and to their mother, and convinced him that they were really his own sons.

The king was exceedingly angry when he heard all the cruel things his stepmother had done, and he gave orders that she should be burnt to death. He then went with the two golden-haired princes to the miserable dungeon wherein his unfortunate wife had been confined so many years, and brought her once more into her beautiful palace. There, looking on her golden-haired sons, and seeing how much the king, their father, loved them, she soon forgot all her long years of misery. As to the king, he felt that he could never do enough to make amends for all the misfortunes his queen had lived through, and all the dangers to which his twins sons had been exposed. He felt that he had too easily believed the stories of the old queen, because he would not trouble himself to inquire more particularly into the truth or falsehood of the strange things she had told him.

After all this mortification, and trouble, and misery, everything came right at last. So the king and his wife, with their golden-haired twins, lived together long and happily.

THE DREAM OF THE KING'S SON.

THERE was once a king who had three sons. One evening, when the young princes were going to sleep, the king ordered them to take good note of their dreams and come and tell them to him next morning.

So, the next day the princes went to their father as soon as they awoke, and the moment the king saw them he asked of the eldest, 'Well, what have you dreamt?'

The prince answered, 'I dreamt that I should be the heir to your throne.'

And the second said, 'And I dreamt that I should be the first subject in the kingdom.'

Then the youngest said, '*I* dreamt that I was going to wash my hands, and that the princes, my brothers, held the basin, whilst the queen, my mother, held fine towels for me to dry my hands with, and your majesty's self poured water over them from a golden ewer.'

The king, hearing this last dream, became very angry, and exclaimed, 'What! I — the king — pour water over the hands of my own son! Go away this instant out of my palace, and out of my kingdom! You are no longer my son.'

The poor young prince tried hard to make his peace with his father, saying that he was really not to be blamed for what he had only dreamed; but the king grew more and more furious, and at last actually thrust the prince out of the palace.

So the young prince was obliged to wander up and down in different countries, until one day, being in a large forest, he saw a cave, and entered it to rest. There, to his great surprise and joy, he found a large kettle full of Indian corn, boiling over a fire and, being exceedingly hungry, began to help himself to the corn. In this way he went until he was shocked to see he had nearly eaten up all the maize, and then, being afraid some mischief would come of it, he looked about for a place in which to hide himself. At this moment, however, a great noise was heard at the cave-mouth, and he had only time to hide himself in a dark corner before a blind old man entered, riding on a great goat and driving a number of goats before him.

The old man rode straight up to the kettle, but as soon as he found that the corn was nearly all gone, he began to suspect some one was there, and groped about the cave until he caught hold of the prince.

'Who are you?' asked he sharply; and the prince answered, 'I am a poor, homeless wanderer about the world, and have come now to beg you to be good enough to receive me.'

'Well,' said the old man, 'why not? I shall at least have some one to mind my corn whilst I am out with my goats in the forest.'

So they lived together for some time; the prince remaining in the cave to boil the maize, whilst the old man drove out his goats every morning into the forest.

One day, however, the old man said to the prince, 'I think you shall take out the goats to-day, and I will stay at home to mind the corn.'

This the prince consented to very gladly, as he was tired of living so long quietly in the cave. But the old man added, 'Mind only one thing! There are nine different mountains, and you can let the goats go freely over eight of them, but you must on no account go on the ninth. The Vilas (*fairies*) live there, and they will certainly put out your eyes as they have put out mine, if you venture on their mountain.'

The prince thanked the old man for his warning, and then, mounting the great goat, drove the rest of the goats before him out of the cave.

Following the goats, he had passed over all the mountains to the eighth, and from this he could see the ninth mountain, and could not resist the temptation he felt to go upon it. So he said to himself, 'I will venture up, whatever happens!'

Hardly had he stepped on the ninth mountain before the fairies surrounded him, and prepared to put out his eyes. But, happily a thought came into his head, and he exclaimed, quickly, 'Dear Vilas, why take this sin on your heads? Better let us make a bargain, that if you spring over a tree that I will place ready to jump over, you shall put out my eyes, and I will not blame you!'

So the Vilas consented to this, and the prince went and brought a large tree, which he cleft down the middle almost to the root; this done, he placed a wedge to keep the two halves of the trunk open a little.

When it was fixed upright, he himself first jumped over it, and then he said to the Vilas, 'Now it is your turn. Let us see if you can spring over the tree!'

One Vila attempted to spring over, but the same moment the prince knocked the wedge out, and the trunk closing, at once held the Vila fast. Then all the other fairies were alarmed, and begged him to open the trunk and let their sister free, promising, in return, to give him anything he might ask. The prince said, 'I want nothing except to keep my own eyes, and to restore eyesight to that poor old man.' So the fairies gave him a certain herb, and told him to lay it over the old man's eyes, and then he would recover his sight. The prince took the herb, opened the tree a little so as to let the fairy free, and then rode back on the goat to the cave, driving the other goats before him. When he arrived there he placed at once the herb on the old man's eyes, and in a moment his eyesight came back, to his exceeding surprise and joy.

Next morning the old man, before he drove out his goats, gave the prince the keys of eight closets in the cave, but warned him on no account to open the ninth closet, although the key hung directly over the door. Then he went out, telling the prince to take good care that the corn was ready for their suppers.

Left alone in the cave, the young man began to

wonder what might be in the ninth closet, and at last he could not resist the temptation to take down the key and open the door to look in.

What was his surprise to see there a golden horse, with a golden greyhound beside him, and near them a golden hen and golden chickens were busy picking up golden millet-seeds.

The young prince gazed at them for some time, admiring their beauty, and then he spoke to the golden horse, 'Friend, I think we had better leave this place before the old man comes back again.'

'Very well,' answered the golden horse, 'I am quite willing to go away, only you must take heed to what I am going to tell. Go and find linen cloth enough to spread over the stones at the mouth of the cave, for if the old man hears the ring of my hoofs he will be certain to kill you. Then you must take with you a little stone, a drop of water, and a pair of scissors, and the moment I tell you to throw them down you must obey me quickly, or you are lost.'

The prince did everything that the golden horse had ordered him, and then, taking up the golden hen with her chickens in a bag, he placed it under his arm, and mounted the horse and rode quickly out of the cave, leading with him, in a leash, the golden greyhound. But the moment they were in the open air the old man, although he was very far off, tending his goats on a distant mountain, heard the clang of the golden hoofs, and cried to his great goat, 'They have run away. Let us follow them at once.'

In a wonderfully short time the old man on his great goat came so near the prince on his golden horse, that the latter shouted, 'Throw now the little stone!'

The moment the prince had thrown it down, a high rocky mountain rose up between him and the old man and before the goat had climbed over it, the golden horse had gained much ground. Very soon, however, the old man was so nearly catching them that the horse shouted, 'Throw, now, the drop of water!' The prince obeyed instantly, and immediately saw a broad river flowing between him and his pursuer.

It took the old man on his goat so long to cross the river that the prince on his golden horse was far away before them; but for all that it was not very long before the horse heard the goat so near behind him that he shouted, 'Throw the scissors.' The prince threw them, and the goat, running over them, injured one of his forelegs very badly. When the old man saw this, he exclaimed, 'Now I see I cannot catch you, so you may keep what you have taken. But you will do wisely to listen to my counsel. People will be sure to kill you for the sake of your golden horse, so you had better buy at once a donkey, and take the hide to cover your horse. And do the same with your golden greyhound.'

Having said this, the old man turned and rode back to his cave; and the prince lost no time in attending to his advice, and covered with donkey-hide his golden horse and his golden hound.

After travelling a long time the prince came unawares

to the kingdom of his father. There he heard that the king had had a ditch—three hundred yards wide and four hundred yards deep—dug, and had proclaimed that whosoever should leap his horse over it, should have the princess, his daughter, for wife.

Almost a whole year had elapsed since the proclamation was issued, but as yet no one had dared to risk the leap. When the prince heard this, he said, "I will leap over it with my donkey and my dog!' and he leapt over it.

But the king was very angry when he heard that a poorly dressed man, on a donkey, had dared to leap over the great ditch which had frightened back his bravest knights; so he had the disguised prince thrown into one of his deepest dungeons, together with his donkey and his dog.

Next morning the king sent some of his servants to see if the man was still living, and these soon ran back to him, full of wonder, and told him that they had found in the dungeon, instead of a poor man and his donkey, a young man, beautifully dressed, a golden horse, a golden greyhound, and a golden hen, surrounded by golden chickens, which were picking up golden millet-seeds from the ground.

Then the king said, 'That must be some powerful prince.' So he ordered the queen, and the princes, his sons, to prepare all things for the stranger to wash his hands. Then he went down himself into the dungeon, and led the prince up with much courtesy, desiring to make thus amends for the past ill-treatment.

The king himself took a golden ewer full of water, and poured some over the prince's hands, whilst the two princes held the basin under them, and the queen held out fine towels to dry them on.

This done, the young prince exclaimed, 'Now, my dream is fulfilled;' and they all at once recognised him, and were very glad to see him once again amongst them.

THE THREE BROTHERS.

THERE was once upon a time an old man whose family consisted of his wife, three sons, and a daughter. They were exceedingly poor, and finding that they could not possibly all live at home, the three sons and the daughter went out into the world in different directions to find some means of living. Thus the old man and his wife remained alone.

Having neither horses nor oxen, the old man was obliged to go every day to the forest for fuel, and carry home the firewood on his back.

On one occasion it was nearly evening when he started to go to the forest, and his wife, who was afraid to remain alone in the house, begged very hard to be permitted to go with him. He objected very much at first, but as she persisted in her entreaties, he at length consented to her following him, first bidding her, however, take good care to make the house-door safe, lest some one should break into the house.

The old woman thought the door would be safest if she took it off its hinges, and carried it away on her back. So she took it off and followed her husband as fast as she was able. The old man, however, was not angry when he saw how she had mistaken his words, and the manner she had chosen to make sure of the door; for, he reflected, there was little or nothing at all in the house for any one to steal.

When they had reached the forest the husband began to cut wood, and his wife gathered the branches together in a heap. Meanwhile it had got very late, and they were anxious as to how they should pass the night, seeing their own house was so far off that they would be unable to reach it before morning, and there were no houses in the neighbourhood where they could sleep. At last they observed a very tall and widely spreading pine-tree, and they resolved to climb up and pass the night on one of its branches.

The man got up first, and his wife followed him, drawing, with great difficulty, the door after her. Her husband advised her to leave the door on the ground under the tree; but she would not listen to him, and could not be persuaded to remain in the tree without her house-door. Hardly had they settled themselves on a branch, the old woman holding fast her door, before they heard a great noise, which came nearer and nearer.

They were excessively frightened at the noise, and dared neither speak nor move.

In a short time they saw a captain of robbers followed by twelve of his men, approach the tree; the robbers were dressed all alike, in gold and silver, and one of them carried a sheep killed and ready for roasting. When the old man and woman saw the band of robbers come and settle under the pine-tree in which they had themselves taken refuge they thought their time was come, and gave themselves up for lost.

As soon as the robbers had settled themselves, the youngest of them made a fire and put the sheep down to roast, whilst the captain conversed with the others. The sheep was already roasted and cut up, and the robbers had begun with great gaiety to eat it, when the old woman told her husband that she could not possibly hold the door any longer, but must let it fall. The old man begged her piteously not to let it go, but to hold it fast and keep quiet, lest the robbers should discover and kill them. The old woman said, however, that she was so exceedingly tired she could no longer by any possibility hold it. The old man, seeing it was no good talking about it, declared that, as he could not hold his corner of the door any longer when she had let go her corner, it was not worth while to complain, 'since,' as he said, 'what must be must be, and it is no use to be sorry for anything in this world.' Thereupon they both loosened their holds of the door at once, and it fell down, making a great noise—especially with its iron lock—as it fell from branch to branch.

The door made so much noise in falling, that the whole forest re-echoed with the sound.

The robbers, greatly astonished at the noise, and too frightened by the unexpected clashing above their heads to see what was the cause, took to their heels, without once thinking of the roast sheep they left behind, or of any of the treasures which they had brought with them.

One of them alone did not run away far from the spot, but hid himself behind a tree, and waited to see what might come of so much noise.

The old couple, seeing the robbers did not return, came down from the tree, and, being exceedingly hungry, began to eat heartily; the old man all the time praising the wisdom of his wife in throwing down the door.

The robber who had hidden himself, seeing only the old people near the fire, came up to them, and begged to be allowed to share their meal, as he had not eaten anything for the last twenty-four hours. This they permitted, and spoke of all kinds of things, until the old man exclaimed suddenly to the robber, 'Take care! you have a hair on your tongue! Do not choke yourself, for I have no means to bury you here!'

The brigand took this joke in earnest, and begged the old man to take the hair out of his mouth, and he would in return show him a cave wherein a great treasure was hidden. As he was describing the great heaps of gold ducats, thalers, shillings, and other coins which he said were in the cave, the old woman interrupted him, saying, 'I will take the hair out of your mouth, without pay! Only put your tongue out and shut your eyes!' The robber very gladly did as she told him, and she caught up a knife and in a moment cut off a piece of his tongue. Then she said, 'Well, now! I have taken the hair out!' When the robber felt what had been done to him he jumped up and down in pain, and at length ran away without hat or coat in the same direction as his companions had gone, shouting all the time, 'Help! help! give me some plaster!' His companions, hearing imperfectly these words, misunderstood him, and thought he cried to them, 'Help yourselves; here is the police-master!' especially as he ran as if the captain of police with a large force was at his heels. Accordingly, the robbers themselves ran faster and farther away.

Meanwhile the old couple thought it no longer safe to stay under the pine-tree, so they gathered up quickly all the money, whether gold or silver, which they could carry, and hurried back to their home. When they got there they found the hens of the neighbours had pulled off the thatch of their house; they were, however, the less sorry for this, since they had now money enough to build another and a better home. And this they did, and continued to live in their fine new house without once remembering their sons and daughter, who had been wandering about the world already some nine long years.

In the meantime the sons and the daughter had been working each in a different part of the world. When, however, they had been away from their home nine years, they all, as if by common consent, conceived an ardent desire to go back once more to their father's house. So they took the whole of the savings which they had laid up in their nine years' service, and commenced their journeys homewards.

On his travels the eldest brother met with three gipsies, who were teaching a young bear to dance by putting him on a red-hot plate of iron. He felt compassion for the creature in its sufferings, and asked the gipsies why they were thus tormenting the animal. 'Better,' he said, 'let me have it, and I will give you three pieces of silver for it!' The gipsies accepted the offer eagerly, took the three pieces of silver, and gave him the bear. Travelling farther on he met with some huntsmen who had caught a young wolf, which they were about to kill. He offered them, also, three pieces of silver for the animal, and they, pleased to get so much, readily sold it. A little further still he met some shepherds, who were about to hang a little dog. He was sorry for the poor brute, and offered to give them two pieces of silver if they would give the dog to him, and this they very gladly agreed to.

So he travelled on homeward, attended by the young bear, the wolf-cub, and the little dog. As all his nine years' savings had amounted only to nine pieces of silver, he had now but a single piece left.

Before he reached his father's house he met some boys who were about to drown a cat. He offered them his last piece of money if they would give him the cat, and they were content with the bargain and gave it up to him. So, at last, he arrived at his home without any money, but with a bear, a wolf, a dog, and a cat.

Just so, it had happened with the other two brothers. By their nine years' work they had only saved nine pieces of silver, and on their way home they had spent them in ransoming animals, exactly as the eldest brother had done.

The sister, in her nine years' service, had saved only five pieces of money. As she travelled homeward she met with a hedgehog who was buying from a mouse its iron teeth, offering in exchange for them its bone teeth and two pieces of money besides.

When she had listened a while to their bargaining, she said to the mouse, 'My dear little mouse, I offer you the hedgehog's teeth and three pieces of silver besides!'

The mouse instantly agreed to this bargain. So she caught the hedgehog, drew its teeth, and gave them, with three pieces of silver, to the mouse, who gave her in return its iron teeth.

As she went on her journey she began to suspect that the mouse had deceived her. To see if this was so or not she determined to make trial of the teeth, and, going a little aside from the road, she found a thick oak-tree and began to bite at it. It seemed to her that she had hardly begun to gnaw at the tree when it already commenced shaking, and threatened to fall. Seeing this, she was satisfied that she had really got the iron teeth, and so went on her journey quite contented.

Before she reached her father's house she observed a mouse sharpening its teeth upon a stone. So she begged the mouse to lend her the stone, that she might sharpen her teeth also. The mouse, however, refused to do this unless she gave two pence. Without much reflection, she took out her last two pieces of money and handed them to the mouse, which gave her in return the stone to sharpen her teeth with.

R

Then she resumed her journey homeward. As she walked, however, she reflected upon what she should say when her parents and brothers asked her where she had been, and how much she had saved during the nine years she had been from home.

When she reached home she found her three brothers already there with their treasures—that is to say, with their bears, wolves, dogs, and cats. Luckily for her, her brothers did not ask her how much she had saved, for they felt sure that she must have made large savings. They asked her only about her health, and how she had travelled, and were all very glad that they were once again united together as a family.

This joy, however, did not last long. Soon after they had returned, the old father died. Then the three brothers consulted together, and decided to invest part of the money, which their father and mother had got from the robbers, in the purchase of four horses and one grass-field.

But their affairs did not go on very smoothly. One morning, instead of three horses in the stable they found only two; the third horse had been killed. Something had bitten it, sucked its blood, and devoured half of its body! And it was the finest of the three horses which had been killed. After this, the brothers resolved for the future to keep watch every night in the stable. When night came, they consulted as to which of them should first keep guard, and the youngest brother said, '*I* will do so.' Accordingly, after having supped, he went to the stable to sleep there. Just about midnight came into the stable a creature all in white, and jumped at once on the youngest horse and began to gnaw it. When the brother who was watching saw that, he was in a great fright; so much so, indeed, that without stopping to find the doors, he got out through a hole in the roof. Whilst he was thus making his escape, the monster killed the horse, sucked its blood, and ate up half the body.

Next day, when the elder brothers saw what had happened, they made a great lamentation over their loss. At night the eldest brother said to the second, 'Now do you go and keep a good watch it is your horse that is in danger!' So the second brother went at once into the stable and lay down. Again, about midnight, the thing in white came in, and the watcher, as much frightened as his younger brother had been the night before, jumped up and escaped just as he had done. The monster, having bitten the horse, sucked its blood, and ate up half of it.

Next morning, when he saw what had happened, the eldest brother said that *he* would keep guard at night over the remaining horse. So at night he went into the stable, gave his horse plenty of hay, and placed himself in a corner to watch. Again, when it was about midnight, the same creature in white came in. Seeing it coming he was first frightened, but soon rallied his spirits and stood, holding his breath, to see what would follow.

He saw that the thing in white looked something like his sister, and carried in its hand a whetstone.

Coming up to the horse the monster bit it, sucked its blood, and, after having eaten up half the body, left the stable. All that time the eldest brother had remained quiet, never stirring at all. Perhaps he did this from fear; perhaps, however, because he had resolved to be quiet, whatever might happen.

Next morning, when the younger brothers found that the horse had been killed and half devoured, during their eldest brother's watch, they began to laugh and to tease him with his loss. He told them that *he*, however, knew what they did not—who it was that had killed and eaten their horses; but that they must not speak a word about it to any one. He then told them that their own sister had slain their horse, and had sucked the blood. At first they refused to believe this; soon, however, they were convinced that it was true. And the proof came in this way.

One morning the two elder brothers went into the fields to work, and the younger remained at home. Their sister likewise remained at home, without knowing, however, that her youngest brother was also in the house. The eldest brother on going out had directed the youngest to place a kettle with water on the fire to boil, and to keep stirring the fire under it. In case the water should turn to blood he was immediately to open the cellar, let out a little dog, and bid it follow the way which they had taken when they went into the fields.

When the two brothers were gone, the youngest went to walk in the yard, and on coming back heard a great noise and wailing in the house. So he went to the house-door and looked in through the keyhole; and what do you think he saw? His sister had cut her old mother's throat, and was just about to put the body on a spit to roast. On seeing this, he was terribly frightened, and ran to hide himself behind a large tub which stood in the kitchen. Shortly afterward his sister brought the spit out of doors, and put it before the fire to roast, speaking aloud, 'I shall do the same with my three brothers, one after the other, and then I shall remain alone the mistress of the entire property.'

When the roasting was done, she carried the spit with the body into the room, and leaning it against a wall, brought out the whetstone and began to sharpen the teeth.

The moment she went inside the house, the youngest brother jumped up from his hiding-place, rushed to the door, and from the outside watched what she was doing. When he had seen this, he filled the kettle, stirred up the fire, and then hid himself near the furnace. Having sharpened her teeth, his sister ate up the body of her mother, all except the head. After she had finished her meal, taking the head in her hand, she went out to the kitchen. On seeing the fire burning so well, and the kettle filled with water, she became angry, and began to look about to discover whether any one was in the house. Suspecting one of her brothers might be there, she shouted aloud, calling her brothers by their names, and searched everywhere in the house. Luckily, however, she forgot to look by the side of the furnace, where her younger brother lay hidden. Not finding any one in the house, she then took her mother's head in her hand and ran out, following the way her brothers had gone to their work in the fields. As she ran she shouted, 'Wait a little! Don't think you have escaped me!'

The youngest brother, seeing his sister had run away, came out of his concealment to look at the water in the kettle. He saw the water had turned to blood, so he went quickly to the cellar and let out one of the little dogs which his sister feared more than all her brothers.

Having let the dog free, the youngest brother came back to the kettle, to see what would happen to the water on the fire. By this time all the water, which had turned to blood, was boiling quickly, and throwing up a great number of bubbles; these bubbles rose the quicker the nearer the sister came to her two brothers in the field. When she was not more than five steps from them, however, she suddenly heard a noise, as if someone was running behind her; so she turned to look, and, seeing the dog coming, was terrified, and tried to save herself by climbing a tree which was close by. When, however, she caught at a branch, it broke in her hand, and she fell to the ground, and the same instant the dog rushed at her, and bit her into two pieces. The two brothers saw all this, but they were afraid to come near her lest she should again revive and attack them. Soon, however, seeing the dog was tearing her to pieces, they became convinced that she was really dead, so they came to the spot where she was, and took up her body and buried it, together with their mother's head, under the tree by which she had fallen.

After they had done this, the two brothers returned home, and told their youngest brother all that had happened. He, on his part, told them how the boiling water had turned to blood and at first bubbled up quicker and quicker, but how, after some time, it grew quieter, and, at length, turned again to water. Then the three brothers congratulated themselves at having got rid of their terrible sister. A few days later they all went into the fields to bring in the hay which the two elder ones had mown. They found, however, hardly the third part of the hay which they had left. At this they wondered greatly, and looked about to see who had stolen it; but, finding no one, after a little while they took up what was left and returned home.

At length the year, on which all this had happened, passed away. The next year, however, they dared not leave their mown grass unwatched. So they discussed which of them should first keep guard. Each of them offered to do it; but, at last, they agreed that the youngest brother should begin to watch. So he prepared himself, and, at night, went out into the field. Having come there, he climbed up into the tree under which his sister's body and his mother's head lay buried, and resolved to remain there until daybreak. About midnight he heard a great noise and shouting, which frightened him so much that he dared not stir at all. Some creatures came into the field and eat up most of the hay, and what they did not eat they tossed about and spoiled, so that it was fit for nothing. When daylight came, the youngest brother came down from the tree and went home, to tell what he had seen.

So that year they had no hay.

Next year, when hay harvest came, the three brothers took counsel together how to preserve their hay. The second brother now volunteered to watch in the field, and seemed quite sure he would be able to save the hay. Accordingly he went, and climbed into the tree, just as his brother had done the previous year. About midnight three winged horses came into the field with a company of fairies. The winged horses began to eat the newly mown hay, and the fairies danced over it. After the greater part of the hay had been eaten by the horses, and all the rest had been spoiled by the dancing of the fairies, the whole company left the field, just as day began to dawn. The watcher in the tree had witnessed all this; he was, however, too frightened to do anything—indeed, he hardly dared to move. When he went home, he told his brothers all that he had seen; at which they were sad, since this year again they would have no hay.

However, the time passed, and the third summer came on. Again the three brothers cut the grass in their meadow, and consulted together anxiously how they should manage to keep their new hay.

At length it was settled that it was now the turn of the eldest brother to keep watch. If he, also, failed to save the hay, it was agreed that they should divide amongst them the little property which they had left, and go out again, separately, to seek their fortunes in the world, seeing they had no luck in their own country.

As had been agreed upon, the eldest brother now went out into the field at night; but, instead of going up into the tree as his brothers had done, he lay quietly down on a heap of hay, and waited to see what would happen. About midnight he heard a great noise, afar off, and, by-and-by, a troop of fairies, with three winged horses, came straight towards the place where he lay. Having got there, the fairies began to dance, and the horses to eat the hay, and canter about. The eldest brother looked on, and, at first, felt much afraid, and wished heartily the whole company would go away without seeing him. As, however, they seemed in no hurry to do this, he considered what he should do, and, at length, decided that it would be worth while to try to catch one of the three horses. So, when they came near him, he jumped on the back of one of them, and clung fast to it. The other two horses instantly ran away, and the fairies with them.

The horse which the eldest brother had caught tried all sorts of tricks to throw off his unwelcome rider, but he could not succeed. Finding all his attempts to free himself quite useless, at last he said, 'Let me go, my good man, and I will be of use to you some other time.' The man answeréd, 'I will set you free on one condition; that is, you must promise never more to come in this field; and you must give me some pledge that you will keep your promise.'

The horse gladly agreed to this condition, and gave the man a hair from his tail, saying, 'Whenever you happen to be in need, hold this hair to a fire, and I will instantly be at your service.'

Thereupon the horse went off, and the eldest brother returned home. His brothers had waited impatiently for his return, and, when they saw him, pressed him immediately to tell them all that had happened. So he told everything, except that he had got a hair from the horse's tail, because he did not believe that the horse would keep his promise and come to him in his need. The two younger brothers, however, had no confidence that the fairies and winged horses would fulfil their promise and never come again to ruin their hay-field, so they proposed that the property should be at once divided, and that they should separate. The eldest brother tried to persuade them to remain at least one other year longer, to see what would happen; he was not able, however, to succeed in this. Accordingly they divided the remnant of their property, took each their animals, that is, each his bear, his wolf, his dog, and his cat, and left their home, for the second time, to seek their fortunes in the world.

The first day they travelled together, but the second day they were obliged to separate, because having come to a crossway, and trying to keep on the same path, they found they could not take a step forward so long as they were together. They therefore left that path and tried another; it was, however, of no use, for they could not move a step forward as long as they were together; and when they tried the third path, the same happened there also. So they tried if two of them could go on in one road if one of them went before and the other behind. But this also they were unable to do; they could not get on one step, try as hard as they would, so nothing was left them but to separate and each of them to go alone by a different road. They were exceedingly sorry to part, but could not help themselves.

Before the brothers separated, the eldest brother said, 'Now, brothers, before we part, let us stick our knives in this oak-tree; as long as we live our knives will remain where we stick them; when one of us dies, his knife will fall out. Let us, then, come here every third year to see if the knives are still in their places. Thus we shall know something, at least, about each other.' The other two agreed to this, and, having stuck their knives in the oak-tree, and kissed each other, went, each one his own way, taking his animals with him.

Let us first follow the youngest brother in his wanderings. He travelled, with his attendant animals, all that day and the following night without stopping, and the next day saw before him a king's palace, and went straight towards it. Having been taken into the presence of the king, he begged his majesty to employ him in watching his goats. The king consented to take him as goat-herd, and from that day he had the charge of the king's goats and lived on thus quietly for a long time.

One day the new goat-herd chanced to drive his flock to a high hill, not far from the king's palace. On the summit of the hill there was a very tall pine-tree, and the instant he saw it he resolved to climb up and look about from its top on the surrounding country. Accordingly, he climbed up, and enjoyed exceedingly the extensive and beautiful prospect. As he looked in one direction he saw, a long way off, a great smoke arising from a mountain. The moment he saw the smoke he fancied that one of his brothers must be there, as he thought it unlikely that any one else would be in such a wilderness. So he resolved at once to give up his place of goat-herd, and travel to the mountain which he had seen in the distance. Coming down from the tree, therefore, he immediately collected his goats, which was a very easy task for him to do, since he had such good help in his bear, his wolf, his dog, and his cat.

No sooner had he reached the palace than he went straight to the king and said, 'Sir, I can no longer be your Majesty's goat-herd. I must go away, for I saw to-day a smoking mountain, and I believe that one of my brothers is there, and I wish to go and see if this be so. I therefore beg your Majesty to pay me what you owe me, and to let me go!' All this time he thought the king knew nothing about the smoking mountain.

When he had said this, however, the king immediately began to advise him on no account to go to the mountain—for, as he assured him, whoever went there never came back again. He told him that all who had gone thither seemed at once to have sunk into the earth, for no one ever heard anything more about them. All the king's warnings and counsels, however, availed nothing; the goat-herd was bent on going to the smoking mountain, and looking after his two brothers.

After he had made all preparations for the journey he set out, accompanied, as usual, by his four animals. He went straight to the mountain; but, having got there, he could not at first find the fire. Indeed, he had trouble enough before he discovered it. At length, however, he found a large fire burning under a beech-tree, and went near it to warm himself. At the same time he looked about on all sides to see who had made the fire. After looking about some time he heard a woman's voice, and upon his looking up to see whence the sound came, he saw an old woman sitting on one of the branches above his head. She sat huddled together all of a heap, and shaking with cold.

No sooner had he discovered her than the old woman begged him to allow her to come down to the fire and warm herself a little. So he told her she might come down and warm herself as soon as she pleased. She answered, however, 'Oh, my son, I dare not come down because of your company. I am afraid of the animals you have with you—your bear, and wolf, and dog, and cat.'

At this he tried to re-assure her and said, 'Don't be afraid! They will do you no harm.' However she would not trust them, so she plucked a hair from her head, and threw it down, saying, 'Put that hair on their necks and then I shall not be afraid to come down.'

Accordingly the man took the hair and threw it over his animals, and in a moment the hair was turned into an iron chain which kept his four-footed followers bound fast together.

When the old woman saw that he had done as she desired, she came down from the tree and took her place by the fire. She seemed at first a very little woman; as she sat by the fire, however, she began to grow larger. When he saw this he was greatly astonished, and said to her, 'But, my old woman, it seems to me that you grow bigger and bigger!' Thereupon she answered, shivering, 'Ha! ha! no, no, my son! I am only warming myself!' But, nevertheless, she continued to grow taller and taller, and had already grown half as tall as the beech-tree. The goat-herd watched her growing with wide-open eyes, and, beginning to get frightened, said again, 'But really you are getting a fearful size, and are growing taller and taller every moment.'

'Ha, ha, my son,' she coughed and shivered, 'I am only warming myself!' Seeing, however, that she was now as tall as the tallest beach-tree, and, fearing that his life was in danger, he called anxiously to his companions, 'Hold her fast, my bear! Hold her fast, my wolf! Hold her fast, my dog! Hold her fast, my cat!' But it was all in vain that he called to them; none of them could move a step from their places. When he saw that, he endeavoured to run away, but found that he could no more move from his place than if he were fast chained to it. Then the old woman, seeing everything had gone on just as she wished, bent down a little, and, touching him with her little finger, said, 'Go, you have lost your head!' and the selfsame moment he turned to ashes. After that, she touched, with the little toe of her left foot, all his animals, one after the other, and they also turned at once to ashes as their master had done.

Having collected all the ashes she buried them under an oak-tree. Then as soon as she took the iron chain in her hand, it turned again into a hair, which she put back into its place on her head.

She had before done with many young and noble knights just as she had now done with this poor goatherd.

The second brother, after serving a long time in a strange place, was seized with a great desire to go to the oak-tree at the cross-roads, where he had parted with his brothers, in order to see if their knives were still sticking in the tree. When he got there, he found the knife of his eldest brother still firmly fixed in the trunk of the oak, but his youngest brother's knife had fallen to the ground. Then he knew that his younger brother was dead, or in great danger of death, and he resolved at once to follow the way he had gone and try to discover what had become of him. Going then along the same road which his younger brother had travelled, he came, on the third day, to the king's palace, and went in and begged the king to take him into his service. Whereupon the king took him as goat-herd, exactly as he had taken before the youngest brother.

When the second brother had tended the king's goats a long time, he one day drove them up a high hill, and, finding there a very tall pine-tree, resolved at once to climb up to its top and look about to see what kind of a country lay on the other side of the hill. When he had looked round a while from the tree he noticed a great volume of smoke rising from a mountain afar off, and the thought came at once to his mind that his brothers might be there. Accordingly, he came down quickly, collected his goats, and went back to the king's palace, followed by his four companions, that is to say, by his bear, his wolf, his dog, and his cat. When he had reached the palace he went straight to the king, and begged him to pay him his wages at once, and to let him go to look after his brothers; for he had seen a smoke upon a mountain, and he believed they were there. The king tried in vain to dissuade him by telling him that none who went there ever came back; but all his Majesty's words availed nothing. Thereupon, seeing he was decided on going, the king paid him what he owed him, and let him go.

He at once set out, and went straight to the mountain; but, when he got there, he was a long time before he could find any fire. At last, however, he found one burning under a beech-tree, and he went up to it to warm himself, wondering all the time who had made it, since he saw no one near. As he warmed himself he heard a woman's voice in the tree above his head, and, looking up, saw there an old woman huddled up on a branch, and shaking with cold.

As soon as he saw her, the old woman asked him to let her come down and warm herself by the fire, and he told her she might come and warm herself as long as she liked.

She said, however, 'I am afraid of the company which you have with you. Take this hair and lay it over your bear, and wolf, and dog, and cat, and then I shall be able to come down.'

So saying, she pulled a hair out of her head and threw it down. He laughed at her fears, and assured her that his companions would not hurt her; finding, however, notwithstanding all he said, that she was still afraid to come down from the tree, he, at last, took the hair and laid it on the beasts as she had directed. In an instant the hair turned into an iron chain, and bound the four animals fast together. Then the old woman came down, and took a place by the fire to warm herself. As the second brother watched her warming herself, he saw her grow bigger and bigger, until she had grown half as tall as the beech-tree.

Wondering greatly, he exclaimed, 'Old woman, you are growing bigger and bigger.' 'Hy, hy! my son,' said she, coughing and shivering, 'I am only warming myself.' But when he saw that she was already as tall as the beech-tree, he became frightened, and called to his companions, 'Hold her, my bear! hold her, my wolf! hold her, my dog! hold her, my cat!' They were none of them, however, able to move, so fast were they held together by the iron chain.

Seeing that, the old woman stooped down and touched him with her little finger, and he fell immediately into ashes. Then she touched the four animals, one after the other, with the little toe of her left foot, and they, also, crumbled to ashes.

No sooner had the old woman done this than she collected all the ashes in a heap and buried them under an oak-tree. As she had before done with the ashes of many a youthful knight and gentleman, so she did now with those of this poor simple man. Pity, if they were to die, that some more worthy means than one hair from the head of a miserable old woman had not brought about their deaths!

A very long time had passed, and yet the eldest brother never once thought of going back to the cross-roads where he had parted with his brothers. He was engaged in the service of a good and honest master, and, finding himself so well off, fancied that his brothers were the same. His master was an innkeeper, and the whole work of the servant was to prepare, morning and evening, the beds of the guests. He did his duty so well that his master thought of adopting him for his son, as he himself was childless.

One day a gentleman of great distinction came to pass the night at the inn, and the servant thought that the stranger looked remarkably like his youngest brother. He wished to ask him his name, but could not for shame; partly because he feared his brother would reproach him for having forgotten to go to the cross-roads; partly because the guest's manners were so polished and his clothes were of fine silk and velvet; whereas he had left his brother very poorly clad, and of rustic manners.

As he thought of the likeness which the guest bore to his youngest brother, he considered that, in his travels about the world, his brother might have found wisdom, and by his wisdom might have succeeded in some way of business, and by his business might have gained money; and then, having got money, that it would be easy for him to get as fine clothes as the stranger wore. Reasoning thus, he took courage at last to ask the gentleman about his family, and at length grew bold enough to ask him plainly if he was not his brother.

This, however, the stranger quickly and positively denied, and asked, in return, about the servant's family. To all the particulars which the servant gave him he listened with a smile.

Next morning, the guest left the inn very early; and when the servant went to arrange the bed in which he had slept, he found, under the pillow, a little stone.

He thought the stone must be valuable, having been in the possession of so rich a man, and yet he considered its loss could hardly be felt by one who went clothed in silks and velvets. He lifted it to his lips to kiss it, before putting it in his pocket; but the moment his lips touched it, two negroes started out and asked him, 'What are your orders, sir?' He was frightened by the suddenness of their appearance, and answered, 'I do not order anything.' Then the negroes disappeared, and he put the stone in his pocket.

The more he thought of this, the more he marvelled at the wonderful stone, and considered what he should do with it. By-and-by, in order to find out what the negroes could do, he took the stone out of his pocket, and raised it again to his lips. The moment he did so, the negroes re-appeared, and asked him again, 'What do you demand, sir?' He replied quickly, 'I desire to have the finest clothes prepared for me, of which no two pieces must be made from the same kind of stuff.' In a very few moments the negroes brought him the most beautiful clothes possible; so fine indeed were they all, that he could not decide which piece was the most beautiful. Then, dismissing the negroes, who disappeared in the stone, he dressed himself. He was admiring the fine fit of his clothes, when his master came to the door of his room, and, seeing a stranger in such an exceedingly rich dress, said humbly, 'Excuse me, sir, where do you come from?'

'From not far off,' the servant answered.

'Wait a moment, sir,' said the innkeeper; 'I will call my servant to take your orders;' and, going outside, he called loudly for his servant.

Meanwhile, the servant quickly threw off his fine clothes and gave them back to the negroes. Dressing himself hurriedly in his old clothes, he rushed out of his room. Then, finding the pantry open, he began to arrange the things.

His master found him employed in this way, and ordered him at once to leave that business, and to go into the house to make coffee for a distinguished guest who had that moment arrived.

The strange guest, however, was nowhere to be found. The innkeeper looked, with his servant, into all the rooms, but there was no sign of a guest anywhere. Then the master, greatly astonished, thought that some thieves had been playing him a trick, and bid the servant in future to look more sharply who came in and who went out of the inn. The servant listened quietly to his master; but, having once remembered his brothers, he had now an irresistible desire to look after them, and so he told the innkeeper that he had resolved to go away, and desired that he might be paid his wages.

The innkeeper was very sad at hearing this, and offered to raise his wages, and tried all means to keep him; but it was of no use. Seeing that the servant was resolved to go away, the master then paid him, and let him leave the inn. Then the eldest brother took with him his four animals—his bear, wolf, dog, and cat, and went away.

After travelling a very long time, his good fortune brought him to the cross-roads where he had parted with his brothers. Instantly he rushed to the oak to see if the knives were still sticking in it, but his own knife alone stood in the tree. The two others had fallen out, and he was much grieved at this, believing that his brothers were dead or that they were in great danger. In his trouble he had quite forgotten the wonderful hair and stone which he possessed. He resolved to go and search after his brothers, and therefore went along the same road his youngest brother had taken when they parted.

As he travelled he remembered the hair which the winged horse had given him, and the stone which he had found at the inn; but these did not much console him, he was so exceedingly sorry for his brothers. After travelling some time he found himself before a large palace, the door-keepers of which asked him if he would take charge of the king's goats. He said he would, if the king could only tell him something about his two brothers, who had travelled that way with a similar company to that which he had. The king said that no men with such a company had passed that way during his reign; and this was quite true, inasmuch as he had only recently mounted the throne, the old king, under whom the two brothers had served, having lately died. However, though the eldest brother could learn nothing of his two younger brothers, he decided to stay some time there, and so engaged himself to the king as goat-keeper.

As he drove the goats out, day by day, he looked about on all sides for some trace of his brothers; for, although their knives had fallen out of the oak-tree, he tried to believe that they were not dead.

One day, as he thus wandered about with his goats, he met an old man, who was going to the forest, with his axe on his shoulder, to cut wood.

So he asked him if he had seen anything of his two brothers. The old man answered, 'Who knows?

Perhaps they have been lost on that mountain where so many other men have lost their lives. Drive your goats up that high hill; from its top you will see a much higher mountain, which smokes, and never ceases to smoke. On that mountain many people have been lost; perhaps your brothers also have perished there. I will, however, give you one piece of good advice. Do not go, for anything in the world, to the place where it smokes. I am now an old man, but I never remember to have seen one man return who went there. Therefore, if your life is dear to you, do not go up that mountain.' So saying the old man went off.

The goat-keeper drove his goats up the hill, and, from its top he saw, as he had been told, a very high mountain which smoked. He tried to discover if any living creature was thereon, but he could not see the traces of a single one there. He considered within himself whether he should go there or not, and, after revolving it over in his mind, he at length determined to go.

In the evening, when he drove the goats home, he told the king of his intention. The king tried hard to dissuade him, and promised to raise his wages if he would stay with him; however, nothing could turn him from his resolution. So the king paid him, and he went away.

Having come to the mountain he found the fire, and wondered who lit it. As he thought over this he heard a woman's voice, saying, 'Hy, hy!' So he looked up, and was astonished at seeing, in the branches of the beech-tree over his head, an old woman huddled together. Her hair was longer than her body, and as white as snow. When he looked up, she said to him, 'My son, I am so cold. I should like to warm myself, but I am afraid of your beasts. I made that fire myself, but, seeing you coming with your animals, I was frightened, and got up here to save myself.'

'Well, you can now come down again, and warm yourself as much as you please,' said he. However, she protested, 'I dare not—your beasts would bite me. But I will throw you a hair, and you shall bind them with it. *Then* I can come down.' The eldest brother thought to himself: the hair must be a very singular hair indeed, if it could bind his bear, his wolf, his dog, and his cat. So, instead of throwing it over the animals, he threw it into the fire. Meanwhile the old woman came down from the tree, and they both sat by the fire. But he never moved his eyes from her.

Very soon she began to grow, and grow, and in a short time she was ten yards high. Then he remembered the words of the old wood-cutter, and trembled. However, he only said to her, 'How you are growing, auntie.' 'Oh, no, my son,' she answered, 'I am only warming myself.' She still grew taller and taller, and had grown as tall as the beech-tree, when he again exclaimed, 'But how you *are* growing, old woman!'

'Oh, no, my son. I am only warming myself,' she repeated as before.

But he saw that she meant him mischief, so he shouted to his companions, 'Hold her, my dog! hold her, my little bear! hold her, my little wolf! hold her, my pussy!' Thereupon they all jumped on the old woman, and began to tear her. Seeing she was unable to help herself, she begged him to save her from her furious enemies, and promised she would give him whatever he asked. 'Well,' said he, 'I demand that you bring back to life my two brothers, with their companions, and all those you have destroyed. Besides that, I demand ten loads of ducats. If you will not comply with these demands, I shall leave you to be torn to pieces by my animals.' The old woman agreed to do all this, only she begged hard that one man should not be brought back to life, because she had said, when she had turned him to ashes, 'When *you* arise, may *I* lie down in your place!' and, therefore, she was afraid she should be turned to ashes herself if *he* came back to life.

As the eldest brother, however, thought that she was trying to cheat him, he would not comply with her request.

Finding that she could not otherwise help herself, she at length said to him, 'Take some ashes from that heap under the tree, and throw them over yourself and your company, and whilst you do so say, "Arise up, dust and ashes—what I am now may you also be!"'

Wonder of wonders! The moment he did as she told him, there arose up crowds of men—more than ten thousand of them. On seeing such a multitude of people coming from under the tree, he was almost struck senseless with astonishment. But he explained to them briefly what had happened. Most of them thanked him heartily; some, however, of them would not believe him, and said with anger, 'We would rather you had not awakened us.' Then they went away in crowds; some took one way, some another, until they were all dispersed. Only his two brothers remained behind; though they, too, for some time could not believe that he was their brother. However, when they saw that their animals recognised his, they remembered that no one but themselves had had such a strange company of beasts. Having recognised each other, the brothers fell into each other's arms, and embraced affectionately. Then they divided the ducats which the old woman had given to the eldest, loaded their animals with their treasures, and went straight away towards the place where they were born, and where their parents had died.

As for the old woman, when the last man arose from the ashes under the oak-tree, she herself crumbled into ashes under it.

The three brothers built three fine palaces for themselves, and lived therein some time unmarried. At length, however, they began to think what would become of all their property after their deaths, and said to each other that it would be a pity for them to die without heirs. So they resolved to marry, that their wealth might be left to their sons and daughters.

The eldest brother said, 'Let me go and find the best wives I can for all three of us; meantime you two will remain here, and take care of our property.' The others gladly agreed to this, as the eldest brother had given proofs enough that he was by far the wisest of the three, and they felt sure that he would be able also to bring this important business to a successful issue. So he made the needful preparations, and started on his journey to look out for three wives for himself and the two younger brothers who remained at home.

After long travelling he arrived at a large city, and resolved to remain there all night, and to continue his journey in the morning.

It happened that the king of that place had just arranged a horse-race, and promised his only daughter as the prize, and, with her, ten loads of treasure to the winner.

The very evening the eldest brother arrived he heard the public bell-man proclaiming aloud through the streets, that every one who had a horse should come to-morrow to the royal field, and whoever should spring first over the ditch should be rewarded with the king's daughter, and should receive, with her, ten loads of gold.

He listened to the proclamation without saying anything. Next morning he went out into the king's field in order to see the racing, and found there already innumerable horses of all kinds.

A little later came also the princess, the king's daughter, and behind her were brought ten loads of treasures.

When he saw the king's daughter he thought her so exceedingly beautiful that he went instantly a little aside from the crowd to get a better sight of her. He then remembered his wonderful stone. Taking it out he now lifted it to his lips, and immediately the two negroes appeared, and said, 'Master what do you command?' He replied, 'Bring me clothes of silk and velvet, together with precious stones, and ten good horses! and bring them as soon as possible!' He had not winked twice before the negroes had placed before him everything which he had demanded. Then he took out the hair, and striking fire with a flint, held the hair near it. The moment he did this, the same cream-coloured horse that had given him the hair stood beside him, and asked, 'Master, what do you command?' He answered, 'I wish that to-day we leave all the other horses behind us in the race, so that I may gain the king's daughter. Therefore prepare yourself, and let us go at once, as the other horses are now ready for starting.'

The instant he had spoken these words, the cream-coloured horse stood, pawing the earth, ready and eager to begin the race. The man then mounted it, and off they went. The other racers, having started a few moments before, were already pretty far from the starting-point; in an instant, however, he had reached them, and in another had passed and left them far behind. When he reached the ditch—which was a hundred and five yards deep, and a hundred yards wide—the horse made so great a spring that it touched ground some fifty yards beyond the ditch, broad as it was.

Then he rode back and took the maiden, the king's daughter, and, placing her behind him on his horse, carried her off, together with the loads of gold. All the people, seeing this, wondered greatly who the strange knight could be who had left all the best horses so far behind in the race, and had won the beautiful princess, with all her rich treasures.

He rode along until he came to a wood pretty far from the city, and there he let his wonderful horse go until he should want him again. He then took off all his beautiful clothes, and put on his old dress, and in this manner went on with the maiden and the loads of gold.

About evening he arrived at a strange city, and decided to remain there. After he had rested a little while, the people in the inn told him that all day long the city bell-man had proclaimed, that whoever had a good horse should go to-morrow to the horse-race, for the king of the palace had offered his only daughter as a prize, together with a hundredweight of gold and jewels; but that there was a ditch to be sprung over which was three hundred and fifty yards deep and a hundred and fifty yards wide. When he heard this he was greatly pleased, for he was quite sure that he should win this race also.

Next morning, by the help of the little stone and the wonderful hair, he was again dressed in the finest clothes, and mounted on his cream-coloured horse, and so took his place amongst the racers.

Every one wondered from what country this knight came, and were delighted at his rich dress; as for the horse, the people were never tired of admiring it. When the race-horses were arranged for the start he remained purposely behind. He knew well enough that this was of no consequence to him, as in one moment he could reach and pass them all. At length he started, and in a moment distanced the fleetest horse, arriving at the ditch, and leaping over it as if it were nothing. Then, without waiting a minute, he took possession of the king's daughter and her treasures, and went straight to the city where he had left the first king's daughter and her loads of gold.

Taking the two princesses and all the wealth with him, he now thought that it was time for him to go back home. On his way, however, he had the great good luck to come again to a large city, where he resolved to remain during the night. There, also, the public crier had been proclaiming all day long, that the king had determined to give his only daughter and fifteen hundredweight of gold to whoever should win the race which was to be run on the morrow. In this instance, however, the horses would have to leap over a ditch one thousand yards deep and four hundred and fifty yards wide. On hearing this proclamation, the eldest brother became very joyful, for he knew that no racer had any chance of beating his wonderful horse.

On the morrow, therefore, by means of his little stone and the hair, he ordered fifteen horses to be ready, to carry away the treasures he felt sure of winning, and, at the same time, directed the negroes to bring him his fairy courser and dresses so splendid that not even a king could buy them.

Richly dressed in this way, and mounted, as he was, on his marvellous horse, all the world, who had gathered to see the great race, could look at nothing except at him.

When all the racers were arranged for the start, he lingered behind and let them all speed off like falcons. He wished every one to see that he was the last to start, that they might not charge him afterwards with having in any way cheated. When they had already gone pretty far, he started himself, and in a moment he had reached them, passed them, and left them all a long, long distance behind. How could it be otherwise? When did the crow outfly the falcon? Coming to the ditch, he touched the bridle a little, and, in an instant, his horse had leaped over the ditch, and they were safe on the other side. So, without any delay, he took away the maiden, together with all the gold, and went back to the city. Having collected his immense treasures, he now took with him the three princesses, and went straight home. As he travelled along with his company, every one who met him asked him, 'Where are you going? are the girls for sale?' For you see the princesses were exceedingly beautiful. But beyond all others his two brothers, when he reached home, wondered and were delighted at the sight of the three beautiful princesses. They did not rejoice half so much over the great riches he had gained for them as over the marvellous fairness of the kings' daughters whom he had brought to be their wives.

Thus each of the three brothers married a beautiful princess; the eldest brother, however, who had shown himself so much the bravest and wisest of them, married the youngest and most beautiful of the three.

ANIMALS AS FRIENDS AND AS ENEMIES.

ONCE upon a time, a long while ago, there lived in a very far-off country, a young nobleman who was so exceedingly poor that all his property was an old castle, a handsome horse, a trusty hound, and a good rifle.

This nobleman spent all his time in hunting and shooting, and lived entirely on the produce of the chase.

One day he mounted his well-kept horse and rode off to the neighbouring forest, accompanied, as usual, by his faithful hound. When he came to the forest he dismounted, fastened his horse securely to a young tree, and then went deep into the thicket in search of game. The hound ran on at a distance before his master, and the horse remained all alone, grazing quietly. Now it happened that a hungry fox came by that way, and seeing how well-fed and well-trimmed the horse was, stopped a while to admire him. By-and-by she was so charmed with the handsome horse, that she lay down in the grass near him to bear him company.

Some time afterwards the young nobleman came back out of the forest, carrying a stag that he had killed, and was extremely surprised to see the fox lying so near his horse. So he raised his rifle with the intention of shooting her; but the fox ran up to him quickly and said, 'Do not kill me! Take me with you, and I will serve you faithfully. I will take care of your fine horse whilst you are in the forest.'

The fox spoke so pitifully that the nobleman was sorry for her, and agreed to her proposal. Thereupon he mounted his horse, placed the stag he had shot before him, and rode back to his old castle, followed closely by his hound and his new servant, the fox.

When the young nobleman prepared his supper, he did not forget to give the fox a due share, and she congratulated herself that she was never likely to be hungry again, at least so long as she served so skilful a hunter.

The next morning the nobleman went out again to the chase, the fox also accompanied him. When the young man dismounted and bound his horse, as usual, to a tree, the fox lay down near it to bear it company.

Now, whilst the hunter was far off in the depth of the forest looking for game, a hungry bear came by the place where the horse was tied, and, seeing how invitingly fat it looked, ran up to kill it. The fox hereupon sprang up and begged the bear not to hurt the horse, telling him if he was hungry he had only to wait patiently until her master came back from the forest, and then she was quite sure that the good nobleman would take him also to his castle and feed him, and

T

care for him, as he did for his horse, his hound, and herself.

The bear pondered over the matter very wisely and deeply for some time, and at length resolved to follow the fox's advice. Accordingly he lay down quietly near the horse, and waited for the return of the huntsman. When the young noble came out of the forest he was greatly surprised to see so large a bear near his horse, and, dropping the stag he had shot from his shoulders, he raised his trusty rifle and was about to shoot the beast. The fox, however, ran up to the huntsman and entreated him to spare the bear's life, and to take him, also, into his service. This the nobleman agreed to do; and, mounting his horse, rode back to his castle, followed by the hound, the fox, and the bear.

The next morning, when the young man had gone again with his dog into the forest, and the fox and the bear lay quietly near the horse, a hungry wolf, seeing the horse, sprang out of a thicket to kill it. The fox and the bear, however, jumped up quickly and begged him not to hurt the horse, telling him to what a good master it belonged, and that they were sure, if he would only wait, he also would be taken into the same service, and would be well cared for. Thereupon the wolf, hungry though he was, thought it best to accept their counsel, and he also lay down with them in the grass until their master came out of the forest.

You can imagine how surprised the young nobleman was when he saw a great gaunt wolf lying so near his horse! However, when the fox had explained the matter to him, he consented to take the wolf, also, into his service. Thus it happened this day that he rode home followed by the dog, the fox, the bear, and the wolf. As they were all hungry, the stag he had killed was not too large to furnish their suppers that night, and their breakfasts next morning.

Not many days afterwards a mouse was added to the company, and after that a mole begged so hard for admission that the good nobleman could not find it in his heart to refuse her. Last of all came the great bird, the kumrekusha—so strong a bird that she can carry in her claws a horse with his rider! Soon after a hare was added to the company, and the nobleman took great care of all his animals and fed them regularly and well, so that they were all exceedingly fond of him.

One day the fox said to the bear, 'My good Bruin, pray run into the forest and bring me a nice large log, on which I can sit whilst I preside at a very important council we are going to hold.'

Bruin, who had a great respect for the quick wit and good management of the fox, went out at once to seek the log, and soon came back bringing a heavy one, with which the fox expressed herself quite satisfied. Then she called all the animals about her, and, having mounted the log, addressed them in these words:—

'You know all of you, my friends, how very kind and good a master we have. But, though he is very kind, he is also very lonely. I propose, therefore, that we find a fitting wife for him.'

The assembly was evidently well pleased with this

idea, and responded unanimously, 'Very good, indeed, if we only knew any girl worthy to be the wife of our master; which, however, we do not.'

Then the fox said, '*I* know that the king has a most beautiful daughter, and I think it will be a good thing to take her for our lord; and therefore I propose, further, that our friend the kumrekusha should fly at once to the king's palace, and hover about there until the princess comes out to take her walk. Then she must catch her up at once, and bring her here.'

As the kumrekusha was glad to do anything for her kind master, she flew away at once, without even waiting to hear the decision of the assembly on this proposal.

Just before evening set in, the princess came out to walk before her father's palace; whereupon the great bird seized her and placed her gently on her outspread wings, and thus carried her off swiftly to the young nobleman's castle.

The king was exceedingly grieved when he heard that his daughter had been carried off, and sent out everywhere proclamations promising rich rewards to any one who should bring her back, or even tell him where he might look for her. For a long time, however, all his promises were of no avail, for no one in the kingdom knew anything at all about the princess.

At last, however, when the king was well-nigh in despair, an old gipsy woman came to the palace and asked the king, 'What will you give me if I bring back to you your daughter, the princess?'

The king answered quickly, 'I will gladly give you

whatever you like to ask, if only you bring me back my daughter!'

Then the old gipsy went back to her hut in the forest, and tried all her magical spells to find out where the princess was. At last she found out that she was living in an old castle, in a very distant country, with a young nobleman who had married her.

The gipsy was greatly pleased when she knew this, and taking a whip in her hand seated herself at once in the middle of a small carpet, and lashed it with her whip. Then the carpet rose up from the ground and bore her swiftly through the air, towards the far country where the young nobleman lived, in his lonely old castle, with his beautiful wife, and all his faithful company of beasts.

When the gipsy came near the castle she made the carpet descend on the grass among some trees, and leaving it there went to look about until she could meet the princess walking about the grounds. By-and-by the beautiful young lady came out of the castle, and immediately the ugly old woman went up to her, and began to fawn on her and to tell her all kinds of strange stories. Indeed, she was such a good story-teller that the princess grew quite tired of walking before she was tired of listening; so, seeing the soft carpet lying nicely on the green grass, she sat down on it to rest awhile. The moment she was seated the cunning old gipsy sat down by her, and, seizing her whip, lashed the carpet furiously. In the next minute the princess found her- herself borne upon the carpet far away from her husband's castle, and before long the gipsy made it descend into the garden of the king's palace.

You can easily guess how glad he was to see his lost daughter, and how generously he gave the gipsy even more than she asked as a reward. Then the king made the princess live from that time in a very secluded tower with only two waiting-women, so afraid was he lest she would again be stolen from him.

Meanwhile the fox, seeing how miserable and melancholy her young master appeared after his wife had so strangely been taken from him, and having heard of the great precautions which the king was using in order to prevent the princess being carried off again, summoned once more all the animals to a general council.

When all of them were gathered about her, the fox thus began: 'You know all of you, my dear friends, how happily our kind master was married; but you know, also, that his wife has been unhappily stolen from him, and that he is now far worse off than he was before we found the princess for him. *Then* he was lonely; *now* he is more than lonely—he is desolate! This being the case, it is clearly our duty, as his faithful servants, to try in some way to bring her back to him. This, however, is not a very easy matter, seeing that the king has placed his daughter for safety in a strong tower. Nevertheless, I do not despair, and my plan is this: I will turn myself into a beautiful cat, and play about in the palace gardens under the windows of the tower in which the princess lives. I dare say she will long for me greatly the moment she sees me, and will send her waiting-women down to catch me and take me up to her. But I will take good care that the maids do not catch me, so that, at last, the princess will forget her father's orders not to leave the tower, and will come down herself into the gardens to see if she may not be more successful. I will then make believe to let her catch me, and at this moment our friend, the kumrekusha, who must be hovering over about the palace, must fly down quickly, seize the princess, and carry her off as before. In this way, my dear friends, I hope we shall be able to bring back to our kind master his beautiful wife. Do you approve of my plan?'

Of course, the assembly were only too glad to have such a wise councillor, and to be able to prove their gratitude to their considerate master. So the fox ran up to the kumrekusha, who flew away with her under her wing, both being equally eager to carry out the project, and thus to bring back the old cheerful look to the face of their lord.

When the kumrekusha came to the tower wherein the princess dwelt she set the fox down quietly among the trees, where it at once changed into a most beautiful cat, and commenced to play all sorts of graceful antics under the window at which the princess sat. The cat was striped all over the body with many different colours, and before long the king's daughter noticed her, and sent down her two women to catch her and bring her up in the tower.

The two waiting-women came down into the garden, and called, 'Pussy! pussy!' in their sweetest voices;

they offered her bread and milk, but they offered it all in vain. The cat sprang merrily about the garden, and ran round and round them, but would on no account consent to be caught.

At length the princess, who stood watching them at one of the windows of her tower, became impatient, and descended herself into the garden, saying petulantly, 'You only frighten the cat; let me try to catch her!' As she approached the cat, who seemed now willing to be caught, the kumrekusha darted down quickly, seized the princess by the waist, and carried her high up into the air.

The frightened waiting-women ran to report to the king what had happened to the princess; whereupon the king immediately let loose all his greyhounds to seize the cat which had been the cause of his daughter being carried off a second time. The dogs followed the cat closely, and were on the point of catching her, when she, just in the nick of time, saw a cave, with a very narrow entrance, and ran into it for shelter. There the dogs tried to follow her, or to widen the mouth of the cave with their claws, but all in vain; so, after barking a long time very furiously, they at length grew weary, and stole back ashamed and afraid to the king's stables.

When all the greyhounds were out of sight the cat changed herself back into a fox, and ran off in a straight line towards the castle, where she found her young master very joyful, for the kumrekusha had already brought back to him his beautiful wife.

Now the king was exceedingly angry to think that he had again lost his daughter, and he was all the more angry to think that such poor creatures as a bird and a cat had succeeded in carrying her off after all his precautions. So, in his great wrath, he resolved to make a general war on the animals, and entirely exterminate them.

To this end he gathered together a very large army, and determined to be himself their leader. The news of the king's intention spread swiftly over the whole kingdom, whereupon the fox called, for the third time, all her friends—the bear, the wolf, the kumrekusha, the mouse, the mole, and the hare—together, to a general council.

When all were assembled the fox addressed them thus: 'My friends, the king has declared war against us, and intends to destroy us all. Now it is our duty to defend ourselves in the best way we can. Let us each see what number of animals we are able to muster. How many of your brother bears do you think *you* can bring to our help, my good Bruin?'

The bear got up as quickly as he could on his hind legs, and brummed out, 'I am sure I can bring a hundred.'

'And how many of your friends can *you* bring, my good wolf?' asked the fox anxiously.

'I can bring at least five hundred wolves with me,' said the wolf with an air of importance.

The fox nodded her satisfaction and continued, 'And what can *you* do for us, dear master hare?'

'Well, I think I can bring about eight hundred,' said the hare cautiously.

'And what can *you* do, you dear little mouse?'

'Oh, *I* can certainly bring three thousand mice.'

'Very well, indeed!—and you, Mr. Mole?'

'I am sure I can gather eight thousand.'

'And now what number do you think you can bring us, my great friend, kumrekusha?'

'I fear not more than two or three hundred, at the very best,' said the kumrekusha sadly.

'Very good; now all of you go at once and collect your friends; when you have brought all you can, we will decide what is to be done,' said the fox; whereupon the council broke up, and the animals dispersed in different directions throughout the forest.

Not very long after, very unusual noises were heard in the neighbourhood of the castle. There was a great shaking of trees; and the growling of bears and the short sharp barking of wolves broke the usual quiet of the forest. The army of animals was gathering from all sides at the appointed place.

When all were gathered together the fox explained to them her plans in these words:—'When the king's army stops on its march to rest the first night, then you, bears and wolves, must be prepared to attack and kill all the horses. If, notwithstanding this, the army proceeds further, you mice must be ready to bite and destroy all the saddle-straps and belts while the soldiers are resting the second night, and you hares must gnaw through the ropes with which the men draw the cannon.

If the king still persists in his march, you moles must go the third night and dig out the earth under the road they will take the next day, and must make a ditch full fifteen yards in breadth and twenty yards in depth all round their camp. Next morning, when the army begins to march over this ground which has been hollowed out, you kumrekushas must throw down on them from above heavy stones while the earth will give way under them.'

The plan was approved, and all the animals went off briskly to attend to their allotted duties.

When the king's army awoke, after their first night's rest on their march, they beheld, to their great consternation, that all the horses were killed. This sad news was reported at once to the king; but he only sent back for more horses, and, when they came late in the day, pursued his march.

The second night the mice crept quietly into the camp, and nibbled diligently at the horses' saddles and at the soldiers' belts, while the hares as busily gnawed at the ropes with which the men drew the cannon.

Next morning the soldiers were terrified, seeing the mischief the animals had done. The king, however, reassured them, and sent back to the city for new saddles and belts. When they were at length brought he resolutely pursued his march, only the more determined to revenge himself on these presumptuous and despised enemies.

On the third night, while the soldiers were sleeping, the moles worked incessantly in digging round the camp a wide and deep trench underground. About midnight the fox sent the bears to help the moles, and to carry away the loads of earth.

Next morning the king's soldiers were delighted to find that no harm seemed to have been done on the previous night to their horses or straps, and started with new courage on their march. But their march was quickly arrested, for soon the heavy horsemen and artillery began to fall through the hollow ground, and the king, when he observed that, called out, 'Let us turn back. I see God himself is against us, since we have declared war against the animals. I will give up my daughter.'

Then the army turned back, amidst the rejoicings of the soldiers. The men found, however, to their great surprise and fear, that whichever way they turned, they fell through the earth. To make their consternation yet more complete, the kumrekushas now began to throw down heavy stones on them, which crushed them completely. In this way the king, as well as his whole army, perished.

Very soon afterwards the young nobleman, who had married the king's daughter, went to the enemy's capital and took possession of the king's palace, taking with him all his animals; and there they all lived long and happily together.

THE LEGEND OF ST. GEORGE.

ONCE upon a time all the saints assembled in order to divide amongst themselves the treasures of the world. And, in this division, each saint obtained something which satisfied him.

The beautiful summer, with all its wealth of flowers, fell to the lot of St. George: to St. Elias fell the clouds and the thunder; and to St. Pantelija the tempest. St. Peter obtained the keys of heaven: to St. Nicholas fell the seas, and the ships upon them; and to the Archangel Michael fell the right of gathering and guarding the souls of the dying. St. John was chosen to preside over friendship and '*koom-ship*,'* and to the holy Lady Mary the saints committed the charge of the lawless country of the cursed Troyan,† in order that she might bring it

---

* The 'koom' is a sort of godfather or sponsor. See 'Popular Customs of Serbia.'

† In some versions of this poem this 'Troyan' is changed into 'India.' Probably there is here a reference to the theory that the Turks and Troyans were the same people. Knolles, in the opening chapter of his 'General Historie of the Turkes,' says, 'Some, after the manner of most nations. derive them from the Troians, led thereunto by the affinity of the words Turci and Teucri; supposing—but with what probability I know not—the word Turci or Turks to have been made of the corruption of the word Teucri, the common name of the Trojans; as also for that the Turks have of long most inhabited the lesser Asia, wherein the antient and most famous city of Troy sometime stood.'—*Edit.*

to a state of peace, and establish therein the true religion.

About a year had passed away since the saints had thus divided amongst themselves the treasures of the world, when one day the holy Lady Mary entered the assembly, evidently greatly afflicted, and with large tears falling over her white cheeks. She greeted '*in the name of God!*' her brethren the saints, and these gave her back her greeting. Then St. Elias addressed her, saying, '*Our* sister, holy Mary, wherefore are you grieving? Why are you shedding these tears? You are, perhaps, dissatisfied with the lot which fell to you when we divided the treasures?'

But the holy Mary answered, 'My brethren, ye who are the righteousness of God, when you divided the treasures you gave me also a share therein, and therewith I am satisfied. Yet I have good cause, nevertheless, to be sorely grieved. I come but now from the city of the Troyan, and I have been unable to bring it to peace and the true faith. There the young people do not reverence their elders—there the brother challenges his own brother to mortal combat,—there the *koom* is pursuing his *koom* in the law courts,—there the brother intermarries with his own sister, and the *koom* with his *kooma*,—there the holy Sabbath is violated, and, worst of all, there they do not pray to the true God. The people have made to themselves a god of silver, and to this idol do they pray. Now, what can I do, my dear brethren, except to pray that the true God should send his lightnings from heaven to destroy the fortress and fortifications, and to burn down the cities and villages? Then, perhaps, the people of the Troyan country may come to see the great wickedness and repent.'

St. Elias said to her these words, 'Our sister, holy Mary, do not do this thing! Rather let us all pray God to allow us to give some warning to the people—that He orders snow to fall on Mitrovdan, and remain until St. George's day;[*] and another snow to fall on St. George's day, and lie on the earth until Mitrovdan;[†] so that no seeds can be sown, and no ewes can rear their lambs. In this way, perhaps, the pride of the earth may be subdued, and the people brought at last to repentance.'

All the saints approved the proposal of St. Elias, and acted as he had said. Then a great snow fell on Mitrovdan, and remained until St. George's day, and a second snowfall came on St. George's day, and lay on the earth until Mitrovdan. No seed could be sown, therefore, and no lambs could be reared. The people suffered greatly throughout the year; they would not, however, repent and mend their ways. Some of them had part of last year's corn in their garners, and shiploads of grain were brought from countries beyond the seas, and so they got somehow through the year, and went on living just as wickedly as before.

The holy Mary, seeing this, went a second time to

---

[*] 'George's day,' 25th April, O. S.
[†] Mitrovdan, 25th October, O. S.

the assembled saints weeping. After the exchange of the customary greeting, St. Elias asked her what was the reason of her tears, and she told him that she was sorely grieved because the people of the Troyan country, notwithstanding the chastisement they had suffered, still continued living in wickedness. Then the saints resolved to send down a second warning. So they prayed God to send down the curse of the small-pox. Thereupon the small-pox appeared amongst the Troyans, and raged in their country for three full years, carrying off all the strength and beauty of the people, so that only the old remained to cough, and the little babes to cry.

But, when the children grew up, they behaved just as their parents had done, and neither improved nor repented. Weeping bitter tears over her white cheeks, the holy Mary went the third time to the assembly of the saints, and reported how disorderly and madly the people of the Troyan land were still living. She said, it was quite evident that they could not be brought to repentance, and that, therefore, she intended now to pray God to send down his lightnings and destroy the cities and villages.

But St. Elias said again, 'Not so, my dear sister! not so! Let us give them yet a third warning.' So the saints prayed to God for the third warning, and God granted their request.

Next morning, close by the king's palace in the chief city of the Troyans a green lake appeared, and therein was an insatiable dragon feeding on young men and maidens. Every morning, for breakfast, the monster required a young man who had never been wedded; and every evening, for supper, he demanded a youthful and blooming maiden.

This went on for seven years, until, at length, the turn came to the only daughter of the king. Then the queen cried loudly and bitterly, and clasped her arms closely round the neck of her child. Mother and daughter wept together three days, and when the fourth day dawned, the queen fell into a light slumber by her daughter's side. As she slept, she dreamed that a man appeared to her, and said, 'O queen of the Troyan city! do not send your daughter this evening to the lake; but send her to-morrow, when the day dawns, and the sun shines. Tell her, when she goes to the lake, she must bathe her face, and then, turning towards the east, let her call on the name of the true God. She must, however, be careful not to mention the idol of silver. This done, she must wait patiently, ready to accept whatsoever the true God ordereth for her.'

The queen, awakening from her sleep, related at once her dream to her daughter, and impressed on her the necessity of carrying out faithfully her instructions. Weeping bitterly, the king's daughter took leave of her mother at daybreak, begging the queen to forgive her the milk with which she had been nourished in her babyhood. Then she went down to the lake shore, bathed her face, and, turning eastwards, prayed to the true God. This done, according to her mother's instructions, she sat down and awaited whatever might happen to her.

Suddenly there appeared a strange knight mounted on a magnificent charger. He greeted the maiden 'in the name of God!' and, she springing up quickly, returned the greeting courteously. Then the strange knight, seeing she had been weeping, asked what it was that troubled her, and wherefore she sat waiting there alone. In answer to these questions the maiden related the whole sad story of the dragon, and the fearful fate which seemed to await her.

When she had finished her narration, the knight dismounted, and, removing his kalpak from his head, said, 'Now I desire to sleep a little, and I wish you to pass your hand through my hair that I may sleep more pleasantly.' The girl tried to dissuade him from this, lest the dragon should come whilst he slept, and devour him also. She said it would be a pity for him to perish thus needlessly. However, she could not prevail on him to abandon his purpose, and he fell at once into a gentle slumber, and slept as quietly as a young lamb.

Very soon, however, the waters of the lake were agitated, and the terrible dragon appeared coming towards them. Then the unknown knight sprang up quickly into his saddle, and, stretching out his arms, lifted the maiden up and placed her behind him on his charger. This done, with one stroke of his lance, he pinned the dragon down to the bottom of the lake, where it remained bleeding, but not dead.

Then the knight took the girl back to the palace of the king, her father, and the queen, who had been watching anxiously everything that passed, met him at the gate and delivered up to him the keys of the city.

The knight, who was no other than St. George, now walked through the streets of the Troyan city, and, having gathered the people around him, spoke to them thus, 'Listen to me, my children! Pray no more to the idol of silver, pray only to the one true God! And you, young people, reverence your elders. All of you remember that near relatives cannot be permitted to inter-marry. Keep holy the Sabbath, as well as all the other holy days and saint days.' Having thus admonished them, the holy knight ordered that the temple should be opened, and when his commands had been obeyed, he took out of it the silver idol, and melted it into a variety of ornaments. In the place of the silver idol he placed a holy picture, and then consecrated the temple, and it became a church. When this was done, he turned again to the people, and said, 'If you will promise to do as I have told you, I will kill the dragon in the lake; but if you refuse to do what I have asked of you I will let him loose again, and I think he will soon make an end of you.'

Then all the people bowed themselves to the earth before the holy knight, and shouted aloud, 'O good and unknown knight! our brother in God! Deliver us from the dragon in the lake, and we will do and live just as you have counselled us!' Whereupon they received the true faith. When they had so done, St. George returned to the lake, and made the sign of the cross over it with a stick, and at that very moment both the lake and dragon disappeared as if they had never been.

Having done all this, St. George went back to the heavenly kingdom to recount to the saints there assembled the conversion of the Troyan people.

THE END.

The Columbus Printing, Publishing and Advertising Company, Ltd., Amberley House, Norfolk Street, London, W.C.

www.ingramcontent.com/pod-product-compliance
Lightning Source LLC
Chambersburg PA
CBHW022059230426
43672CB00008B/1220